COOLBRANDS TWO-THOUSAND AND EIGHT/NINE

**An insight into some of
Britain's coolest brands**

CoolBrands.uk.com

FSC
Certificate No.
CQ–COC–000012

The paper used for this book has been independently certified as coming from well-managed forests and other controlled sources according to the rules of the Forest Stewardship Council.

This book has been printed and bound in Italy by Printer Trento S.r.l., an FSC accredited company for printing books on FSC mixed paper in compliance with the chain of custody and on-products labelling standards.

TWO-THOUSAND AND EIGHT/NINE

Chief Executive
Ben Hudson

Brand Liaison Directors
Fiona Maxwell
Liz Silvester

Brand Liaison Manager
Heidi Smith

Administrative Co-ordinator
Alice McSeveney

Head of Accounts
Will Carnochan

Managing Editor
Laura Hill

Author
Karen Dugdale

Designer
Claire Boston

2008/09 Creative
Clusta Ltd
www.clusta.com

Other publications from Superbrands in the UK:

Superbrands 2008/09
ISBN: 978-0-9554784-4-4

Business Superbrands 2008
ISBN: 978-0-9554784-3-7

To order these books, email
brands@superbrands.uk.com
or call 01825 767396.

Published by
Superbrands (UK) Ltd
44 Charlotte Street
London
WIT 2NR

© 2008 Superbrands (UK) Ltd

Printed in Italy

ISBN: 978-0-9554784-5-1

AN INSIGHT INTO SOME OF BRITAIN'S COOLEST BRANDS

2008 /09

CONTENTS

ENDORSEMENTS

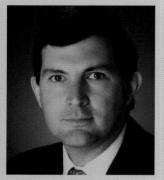

JOHN NOBLE

Director
British Brands Group

The collection of case studies presented here celebrates the rich diversity of branding, demonstrating its relevance to products and services young and old, niche and mass market. Some in this collection had me reaching for Google while others are names etched in my mind, reminding me that brands are deeply personal, none more so than the 'cool' ones.

That brands bring colour, diversity and richness to our lives is clear from these pages and for brands to be considered 'cool' they must connect in a particularly relevant and contemporary way. Building such brands is not easy, requiring acute understanding of how people live their lives, a desire to do things differently and significant investment.

It is not the easy option. The British Brands Group is dedicated to ensuring that the right policy environment exists in the UK to encourage the building of such brands and we are therefore delighted to support this unique and vibrant collection.

Global Marketing Network
The new home of marketing

DARRELL KOFKIN

Chief Executive
Global Marketing Network

Global Marketing Network is committed to raising standards in marketing practice worldwide and to supporting and rewarding the aspirations of the marketer. We are therefore absolutely delighted to support the CoolBrands publication, and the role that it plays in recognising such achievements.

Marketers are playing an increasingly important part in building brands that add both sustainable and demonstrable value to the customer and to society as a whole. To build a 'CoolBrand' requires a further range of complex skills, including an innate ability to have a finger on the pulse of the 'now' while being ever conscious of the 'next'.

We congratulate all those CoolBrands that have made it into this volume, and to those people that have been associated with building them, thank you for inspiring us all through your innovation.

/09

DEREK HOLDER

**Managing Director
The Institute of
Direct Marketing**

Define 'cool'. It's harder than you think. The definition is as elusive as the status itself. But one thing is for sure: it's the customer who decides whether or not a brand is cool. Not the designer, not the manufacturer and certainly not the marketer. In elevating themselves to cool status, the brands within these pages have connected with consumers in a way that most marketers can only dream of. They have not only understood their needs and motivations, but also their psyche. They've understood too the need to be brave enough to hand the balance of power firmly to their customers. And they've reaped the rewards.

The Institute of Direct Marketing is proud to endorse the CoolBrands project once again and we hope that the insights and case studies that follow will not only help define cool but also how to achieve it.

JAMES AITCHISON

**Managing Editor
World Advertising
Research Center**

When I think of 'cool' brands, it's the new and younger brands that typically spring to mind, like those in trendy sectors aimed at the more youthful end of the consumer spectrum – quirky beers, kooky clothing, that sort of thing.

But browse this latest tome of CoolBrands – which assesses cool in an eminently more scientific manner than my musings here – and you'll find brands new and old, young and mature, operating in an equally diverse range of markets.

So yet again, the CoolBrands programme has taught me something important about brands: cool brands are not defined by their age, or by the youth of their consumer, or by the character of their market. What, then, does make a brand cool? To answer that, I strongly recommend you read the pages that follow.

/10

ABOUT COOLBRANDS

CoolBrands is an annual initiative to identify and pay tribute to the nation's coolest brands. Since 2001 we have been canvassing the opinions of experts and consumers to produce an annual barometer of the nation's coolest brands, people and places.

The 2008/09 CoolBrands are celebrated in this book, via a national media supplement and at CoolBrands.uk.com. Each brand featured in this, the seventh annual programme, has qualified for inclusion based on the collective opinions of the independent and voluntary Expert Council and more than 2,500 members of the British public. Full details of the selection process are provided overleaf.

CoolBrands is one of three annual programmes administered by Superbrands (UK) Ltd. Superbrands was launched in London in 1995 and is now a global business operating in more than 55 countries worldwide.

COOLBRANDS STAMP

The brands that have been awarded 'CoolBrand' status and participate in the programme are licensed to use the CoolBrands Award Stamp.

This powerful endorsement provides evidence to existing and potential consumers, the media, employees and investors of the exceptional standing that these CoolBrands have achieved.

AWARDED FOR
UK
CoolBrands
2008/09
INNOVATION · STYLE · DESIRABILITY

VOTED ONE OF THE UK'S COOLEST BRANDS
BY EXPERTS & CONSUMERS

/12

COOLBRANDS SELECTION PROCESS

Each year just 500 CoolBrands are chosen by the Expert Council and members of the British public. Brands do not pay or apply to be considered. The entire selection process is independently administered by The Centre for Brand Analysis. The key stages of the selection process are as follows:

A comprehensive database of the UK's coolest brands is compiled using a wide range of sources, from sector reports to blogs. From the thousands of brands initially identified, approximately 1,100 brands are short-listed. An independent and voluntary Expert Council (see page 14) scores this list, with members individually awarding each brand a rating from 1-10. Council members are not allowed to score brands with which they have a direct association or are in direct competition to.

The lowest-scoring brands (approximately 40 per cent) are eliminated. A nationally-representative group of more than 2,500 UK consumers on the YouGov panel are asked to vote on the surviving brands. The opinions of the Expert Council (70 per cent) and the British public (30 per cent) are combined and the 500 highest-ranking brands are awarded 'CoolBrand' status.

Cool is subjective and personal. Accordingly, voters are not given a definition but are asked to bear in mind the following factors, which research has shown are inherent in a CoolBrand: style, innovation, originality, authenticity, desirability, and uniqueness.

THE CENTRE FOR BRAND ANALYSIS

THE CENTRE FOR
BRAND
ANALYSIS

The Centre for Brand Analysis (TCBA) is dedicated to understanding the performance of brands. Its services aim to allow brand owners, agencies and other organisations to understand how a brand is performing, either at a point in time or on an ongoing basis. TCBA also offers insight into wider market and marketing trends.

TCBA utilises extensive relationships within the business community and works with third parties where appropriate, to access pertinent opinions, data and insights.

EXPERT COUNCIL 2008/09

WALÉ ADEYEMI
Fashion Designer
- Stylist to international A-list stars, and now one of the UK's most recognised and successful fashion designers since emerging on the scene in 1998.
- Has spoken at Oxford University on fashion, is a proud Prince's Trust Ambassador and was awarded an MBE in 2008.
- Combines his day-to-day design work with his new appointment as creative director for American brand, New Era.

NIKU BANAIE
Vice President of Strategy & Innovation, Isobar
- Joined Isobar, one of the world's leading full service digital networks, in June 2008. Prior to this he was the youngest partner at Naked Communications London where he created award-winning work for Honda, Orange, E4 and Nike amongst others.
- Outside of work projects include brothersister – a furniture label that can be found in the V&A.
- Graduated from Central Saint Martins with Distinction.

DAMIAN BARR
Journalist, Writer, Playwright & Presenter
- Writes features and blogs for The Times, The Independent, The Telegraph, Olive and Country Life, as well as plays for BBC Radio 4.
- Presents a radio series for BBC Scotland and fronts Cool In Your Code – a web TV series for The Times.
- His first book made the quarterlife crisis a household term.

ED BARTLAM
Co-Founder & Director, Underbelly Ltd
- Founded Underbelly in 2000 at the Edinburgh Festival, at the age of 19. Growing rapidly from a small scale Fringe venue it is now the third largest venue in Edinburgh.
- Through Underbelly, manages comedians, books comedy for music festivals, and tours the 'upside-down cow' Udderbelly tent to other cities and festivals.
- Won the 'Outstanding Off Stage Contribution' award at the Chortle Live Comedy Awards in 2006.

/15

PATRICK BURGOYNE
Editor, Creative Review

- Worked in marketing – for The Body Shop and the University of Westminster – before joining Creative Review as staff writer, becoming editor in 1999.
- Author of several books on design and visual culture, including 'Bored: Surf, Skate, Snow Graphics' (with Jeremy Leslie).
- Has written for many publications, including The Independent, Scotland on Sunday, Graphis, La Repubblica and The Big Issue.

NEIL BYRNE
Board Director, Camron

- Heads up the architecture division at Camron, the UK's leading design and architecture PR company.
- Has worked on many landmark architectural projects around the world, from China to the Middle East and America to Europe – giving him a global perspective on brands and a firm understanding of what makes a brand cool.
- Currently leads the PR team for The Shard, Renzo Piano's new London Bridge skyscraper.

KATE CREASEY
Editor, Cosmopolitan.co.uk

- An award-winning online journalist and editor of Cosmopolitan.co.uk since November 2007, responsible for bringing the online community a diverse mix of content.
- An authority on web trends and online publishing, with more than nine years' experience as an online editor.
- Prior to a stint as a beauty editor (and indulging a guilty obsession with make-up, creams and potions), career began in fashion, beauty and health PR.

BEN DE LISI
Fashion Designer

- Studied sculpture at the Pratt Institute in Brooklyn before moving to London in 1982 and producing his first capsule collection.
- Has shown at London Fashion Week since 1995, and acted as a mentor on TV's Project Catwalk programme.
- Designs a diffusion line in conjunction with Debenhams – BDL by Ben de Lisi – and opened his first stand-alone boutique in 1998.

GERRY DEVEAUX
Writer, Producer & Style Consultant
- As a songwriter and producer, has worked with Lenny Kravitz, Angie Stone, Chaka Khan and more.
- Contributing editor for Tatler magazine and creative consultant and ambassador for Fashion Rocks for The Prince's Trust.
- Style consultant for MTV, creative director and judge for Britain's Next Top Model, produces and presents Living Style with Gerry DeVeaux on BBC World and teamed up with June Sarpong for Channel 4's Slave to Fashion.

ELEANOR FORSTER
Director, FORSTER
- Launched contemporary art gallery, FORSTER – based in London's Shoreditch – in January 2007; promoting the careers of a core base of artists through an exhibition and art fair schedule in London, Basel and the US.
- Established thecentralhouse and ran the art consultancy business for four years.
- Was head of art consultancy at britart.com, a contemporary art gallery with an online presence.

LEE FARRANT
Partner, RPM Group
- Early career encompassed sports photography, from Formula One and football to the Olympics and Camel Trophy adventure races.
- Joined experiential marketing specialists, RPM, as a partner in 1996 and set up the agency's design and photography offering.
- Combines joint passions of sport and photography with business; currently working with brands such as Diageo, Land Rover, The ECB, The FA, FIFA, Sky TV, Unilever and Royal Ascot.

SANDRA HALLIDAY
Global Managing Editor, Business, Reporting & Analysis, WGSN
- Runs the news, business, celebrity and future analysis side of global intelligence company WGSN, having worked there for nine years.
- An experienced journalist, over the past 25 years has morphed from a fashion editor into a fashion and beauty news and business writer.
- Has been a consultant for special projects within the cosmetics sector, as well as a frequent fashion industry commentator for the media.

NEWBY HANDS
Associate Editor & Director of Health & Beauty, Harper's Bazaar

- Was style & beauty editor at the Daily Mail, before moving to Harper's Bazaar 13 years ago.
- After completing a buying course at Harrods, worked in the music business before moving into fashion and journalism on the London Evening Standard.
- Named 2008's 'Beauty Journalist of the Year' at the P&G Beauty Awards, receiving an Achiever Award from CEW (UK) in the same year.

ANDREW HARRISON
Associate Editor, The Word & Editor-in-Chief, Mixmag

- Founding staffer of new model independent publishers Development Hell Ltd, co-launching The Word and acquiring and revamping Mixmag.
- The first British writer to identify the transformative nature of the iPod, in 'Honey, I Shrunk The Record Collection' (Word, 2003).
- Has written on music and popular culture for Rolling Stone, GQ, Arena, The Face, the Guardian, The Observer and Marie Claire.

JACK HORNER
Co-Founder & Creative Director, FRUKT

- Warner Music UK's first head of new media, prior to establishing a music division for digital design agency AMX and working on a global music venture for Heineken.
- Oversees idea generation, planning and creative direction at specialist music strategy and communications agency FRUKT.
- Publishes monthly music insight magazine Five Eight and a free fortnightly newsletter through www.brandsbandsfans.com.

DOLLY JONES
Editor, VOGUE.COM

- Studied at boarding school in Salisbury, went to boys' school in Oxford, took History of Art at Manchester and went straight to Vogue for work experience.
- On the journalism course at the London College of Arts she was told to interview "someone at the top of their game" – Alexandra Shulman kindly obliged.
- A trusted authority on fashion, VOGUE.COM incorporates a daily news service and coverage of every catwalk show in the world.

KATRINA LARKIN
Co-Founder, The Big Chill
- Formed The Big Chill in 1994 with Pete Lawrence, launching The Big Chill Festival the following year.
- Has staged events in Goa, Cairo and Greece through The Big Chill, and established its record label with an eclectic roster of artists.
- In partnership with The Cantaloupe Group, opened Big Chill Bar off London's Brick Lane in 2005, followed in 2007 by The Big Chill House in Kings Cross.

LAUREN LAVERNE
Radio & TV Broadcaster
- TV presenting credits include The Culture Show for BBC Two, Channel 4's Transmission, The Orange Playlist, CD:UK and a wealth of festival coverage such as Glastonbury for the BBC and the Isle of Wight Festival for ITV.
- Has hosted numerous award ceremonies, including the BRITs and the NME Awards.
- Received a 2006 Sony Radio Academy Award while presenting the Xfm Breakfast Show, and now presents a weekly 6 Music show.

CHRIS LIGHTFOOT
Director, Whitestone International
- Founded Whitestone International in 2000, which specialises in building sports brands for clients including FIFA, The FA, ICC, ECB, IAAF, Olympic Council of Asia, NFL, Manchester City Football Club, Reebok and adidas.
- Is a director of British Universities & Colleges Sport, responsible for marketing, communications, brands and the commercial arm.
- Was creative director at Interbrand from 1990 to 2000, having previously been a designer at Michael Peters.

TREVOR NELSON
DJ
- Started broadcasting career at (the then pirate station) Kiss FM before going on to A&R artists such as D'Angelo and signing Lynden David Hall.
- Hosts the official start to the weekend on Radio 1, a soul and R&B show on Radio 2, the 1 Xtra weekly breakfast show, and presents MTV's The Lick.
- Was awarded an MBE for services to charity, DJs regularly across Europe and has released five compilation albums.

LAURETTA ROBERTS
Editor, Drapers
- Has edited fashion business bible Drapers since the start of 2007, relaunching the magazine and introducing its first content-driven website with daily news service.
- Twelve years' experience in business writing and editing spans sectors from print media and publishing, to live events, design and fashion.
- Acts as a judge for several fashion industry awards and regularly appears in the media as an industry commentator.

NICOLAS ROOPE
Founding Partner, Poke London
- Impassioned digital media visionary with a career spanning 13 years, concluding at Poke as joint-founder and creative director.
- Member of the Academy of Digital Arts and Sciences and UK Webby Ambassador.
- Founder of the cult electronics brand Hulger (www.hulger.com); three products are in MoMA's permanent design collection in New York.

PARDEEP SALL
Editor-at-Large, TRACE Magazine
- Has contributed articles to publications across the globe including Spin, Fortune, GQ, Music Week, Billboard, Wired and Vibe magazines.
- He has worked as a strategic planner for enterprises across various areas of industry.
- As editor of TRACE, was one of the youngest in the business and has a firm grasp on what's new, and more importantly, what's next.

JUNE SARPONG
Presenter
- Began TV career presenting for MTV before joining Channel 4 in 1999 as front-woman for T4, interviewing the likes of Sir Elton John, Kylie Minogue, Will Smith, Nicole Kidman and Tony Blair.
- Has hosted the Smash Hits Poll Winners Party, Party In The Park and the MOBO Awards.
- Is an ambassador for The Prince's Trust, campaigns for Make Poverty History and has received an MBE for services to charity.

TOM SAVIGAR
Partner, The Future Laboratory
- Co-founder of Sense Worldwide prior to joining The Future Laboratory. His team conducts trend research and brand strategy for the likes of Nokia, BMW, Lamborghini and Coke Zero.
- Is passionate about understanding the emotional aspects of consumer behaviour and enabling brands to express their personality.
- Teaches fashion textile students at the University of Brighton and East London.

JESS SEARCH
Chief Executive, Channel 4 British Documentary Film Foundation & BRITDOC Festival
- A Channel 4 commissioning editor for five years before becoming CEO of both the Channel 4 British Documentary Film Foundation and the BRITDOC Festival.
- Co-founded Shooting People, the online filmmakers network dedicating to helping its (37,000 plus) members get their films funded, made and seen.
- Is wearing Albert Maysles' glasses in this photo.

BOB SHEARD
Founder & Creative Director, Fresh
- A stint as creative director for Converse in the mid 1990s was followed by a move to Karrimor, taking on the mantle of creative director once again.
- Founded Fresh in 1997, a multi-discipline agency based in London.
- Clients include Nike, adidas, Rbk, Cat, Wrangler, Sebago, Dr Martens, Salomon and Renault Trucks.

MICHAEL ACTON SMITH
CEO, Mind Candy
- Founder of online games company, Mind Candy, and co-founded online retailer Firebox.com 10 years ago, in a Cardiff attic with £1,000.
- Created Moshi Monsters – the online world of adoptable pet monsters – and invented the Shot Glass Chess Set, a best-selling fusion of chess and alcohol.
- Created Perplex City in 2004, a global treasure hunt with a £100,000 prize.

ROGER WADE
Director, Brands Incorporated

- Runs his own brand consultancy company, Brands Incorporated, specialising in licensing and raising private equity for UK fashion brands – working with major British brands such as Aquascutum, Pentland, JD Sports, asos.com and Timothy Everest.
- Founded the original British streetwear brand, Boxfresh, in 1989 and was the first to import Carhartt into the UK.
- A regular columnist for Drapers magazine.

DYLAN WILLIAMS
Head of Strategy, Mother

- Joined Bartle Bogle Hegarty (BBH) in 1996, was promoted to the board as its youngest ever member in 1999, and then named one of the UK's top two communication strategists by ad industry journal Campaign.
- Now heads up Strategy at Mother and works across all of its major clients including Orange, Motorola and Diageo.
- Is a shareholder and partner in emerging fashion label BSA menswear.

STEPHEN CHELIOTIS
Chairman, Superbrands Councils UK & Chief Executive, The Centre for Brand Analysis

- Began career at Brand Finance, advising companies on maximising shareholder value through brand management.
- Joined Superbrands in 2001, rising to UK managing director before moving on to a European role.
- Left Superbrands to establish The Centre for Brand Analysis – contracted to run the CoolBrands selection process.

Also a member of the
Expert Council:

LISA PAULON
Founder, The Camden Crawl & Managing Director, Traffic Marketing

AUTHENTICITY ORIGINALITY INNOVATION

DESIRABILITY UNIQUENESS STYLE

AGENT PROVOCATEUR

When Agent Provocateur unleashed its vision of lingerie on the world, it set out to free consumers from the British prudery that categorised anything to do with sex as sleazy or smutty.

agentprovocateur.com

Agent Provocateur

Agent Provocateur opened its first boutique in London's Soho in 1994. What followed was a media frenzy reserved usually for superstars; the response was both exceptional and overwhelming.

The aim was to create an availability of high quality designer lingerie with flair to stimulate, enchant and arouse both the wearers and their partners: 'A woman wearing a scrumptious pair of knickers promotes in herself a sexy superhero feeling, which exudes itself as a confident and positive sexuality.'

Agent Provocateur has become a phenomenal success with more than 40 stores worldwide and many more in the pipeline. With select store locations, each boutique is an emporium decorated in a boudoir style, featuring seductive and luxurious furnishings to complement the lingerie and indulge the customer. The carefully handpicked staff wear the famous pink house coat (designed by Vivienne Westwood), which has become a much emulated and iconic glamorous service look. Agent Provocateur has a thriving mail order catalogue and an award-winning website which receives on average more than 20,000 visitors a day.

The Agent Provocateur annual campaign has also become internationally renowned, each offering a groundbreaking creative concept and causing a furore on its launch at the beginning of September. The 2008/09 campaign, 'Tableaux Vivants', opens with 'The Season of the Witch' (pictured on this page). Its creative collaborations also push boundaries, with the 'White Wedding' campaign starring Kate Moss being a key example. The campaign images portray Kate as a beautiful, blushing bride who has a change of heart. She is seen tearing up pictures of a masked man flanked by two screaming popes (played by British artists Jake and Dinos Chapman), with the final shot swathed in black and red and the words 'Let them eat Kate' scrawled across it.

The brand's cinema advertising, catalogues, events, books and additional sensual lifestyle products have all

attracted substantial national and international media coverage, firmly securing Agent Provocateur's place as one of the truly credible lingerie brands on the fashion map and spawning an explosion of lingerie into the fashion world.

Agent Provocateur has always understood the important marriage between scent and seduction, and in 2000 it launched its first fragrance, the signature Eau de Parfum. Presented in an egg-shaped porcelain bottle, the perfume has won the most prestigious of beauty awards – a Fifi award for best fragrance – and has since become a modern classic. In 2007 Agent Provocateur did it again with its second female perfume, Agent Provocateur Maîtresse, winning a Fifi for 'Best New Prestige Female Fragrance'.

At the heart of Agent Provocateur is a profound belief in the intimacy of the experience that it offers,

described by its co-founders as "the difference between a mass experience, dictated by market forces and meaningless advertising, and an intensely private, wholly personal experience". It is an experience that is realised through quality, service and an absolute refusal to adhere to fluctuating trends. As Agent Provocateur enters its 15th year, it remains committed to investment in creativity led by pure instinct of that which is beautiful and of course erotic. Agent Provocateur leads where others will follow.

APRILIA

Combining Italian passion and style with the very best in performance technology for the motorbike and scooter markets, the Aprilia name

Aprilia's origins date back to the end of World War II when Cavalier Alberto Beggio founded a factory in Noale, near Venice, to manufacture bicycles.

Ivano, his son, joined the business in 1968 and with a few Aprilia employees, built the first Aprilia motorbike. It was clear from this point forward where the direction of the brand lay. The initial model was well received by the market, as were Aprilia's first moped designs, but it wasn't until the launch of the Scarabeo cross bike in 1970 that the brand really got noticed. The Scarabeo quickly became the 'must-have' item for those competing in national competitions and heralded the start of a strong affinity between sports and production bikes. The models included metallic gold paintwork, which was to become a feature of all Aprilia products.

During the late 1970s, the factory expanded activities beyond Italy and by 1979 annual production of mopeds went from 150 to 12,000 units, with motorbike production growing to more than 2,000 units per year. Aprilia's commercial success was consolidated during the 1980s, when it became the market leader in motorbikes for the younger generation. During this period its range expanded to include models from 50 to 600cc and the brand took on new challenges in the form of world rallies and the Grand Prix Championship.

The 1990s were equally successful and saw Aprilia become Europe's second largest motorcycle manufacturer, its reputation for cutting-edge design corroborated by the launch of the first scooter to make major use of plastics in its construction. Further innovation followed in 1995, when it joined forces with renowned

designer, Philippe Starck, to build the Moto6.5; a model that broke the mould when it launched and has since acquired a cult following. In 1998, Aprilia successfully entered the larger bike category, launching the RSV Mille, which was awarded 'Superbike of the Year' in 1999. A return to the off-road sector in 2004 resulted in an immediate win at the World Supermoto Championship with the twin cylinder Supermoto SXV5.5, a bike that reiterated Aprilia's passion for technical, sporting and stylistic innovation.

At the end of 2004, Aprilia was acquired by the Piaggio Group. One of the world's leading manufacturers of two-wheeled motor vehicles, and leader in the European market, the Group had a turnover of 1.5 billion euros, production stood at more than 610,000 units annually, and sales were present in over 50 countries. Under the strategic guidance of the Piaggio Group, Aprilia is now on course to strengthen its market position while maintaining and developing its brand identity. Key investment is making way for a refreshed product range, with the first of these new models – the SL 750 Shiver, NA 850 Mana and SMV 750 Dorsoduro – already causing a stir in their specific sectors. 2009 will see the launch of the company's new flagship model, the RS V4. The world's first mass-produced 1000cc V4 Superbike will mark a return to racing for Aprilia in the competitive world Superbike arena, challenging the established Japanese models for supremacy.

While Aprilia's short term objective is to break into the strategic markets of China and India, its primary focus remains unchanged: to produce specialist motorcycles and sophisticated scooters that combine class, innovation and the very best in Italian engine technology.

ASTON MARTIN

Sleek design and attention to detail, with perfectly proportioned flowing bodywork and luxury interiors; an Aston Martin combines power and sporting ability with refinement and aesthetic beauty.

astonmartin.com

ASTON MARTIN

A strong heritage coupled with exceptional quality and craftsmanship has kept Aston Martin at the forefront of car manufacturing and racing for more than 90 years.

Its history dates back to 1914, when racing drivers Lionel Martin and Robert Banford began selling bespoke racing cars. After some early track successes, the focus of the fledgling company – named after the Aston Clinton hill climb course in Buckinghamshire – shifted to powerful road cars, resulting in the launch of the innovative Atom saloon during World War II. Post-war, under the guidance of charismatic new owner, David Brown – and thanks to the DB series of saloons – Aston Martin's reputation really began to take hold; the DBR1's considerable success at world-famous tracks kick-starting the brand's racing pedigree.

In recent years Aston Martin has returned to the track, following the introduction of a brace of specially developed racing cars: the DBR9, DBRS9 and V8 Vantage N24. In both 2007 and 2008, an Aston DBR9 won the GT1 class at Le Mans, evoking memories of the DBR1's classic Le Mans victory in 1959. In May 2008, the V8 Vantage N24 took the top three podium spots in the SP8 class at the famous Nürburgring 24-hour event.

Every model, from the 2005 V8 Vantage to the V12-engined DBS – debuted in 2008 – is produced at the brand's award-winning factory in Gaydon, Warwickshire, by a skilled workforce that combines traditional hand-finishing with high-tech manufacturing techniques. In December 2007, a new purpose-built design studio opened to house the company's design team, led by Marek Reichman. The facility, the first in the brand's history, hosts a number of specially commissioned art installations as part of Aston Martin's commitment to supporting modern art, innovation and creativity.

The brand has a strong cinematic tradition that began in 1964 with Sean Connery's 007 driving a DB5 in Goldfinger. In 2006, a DBS made its debut, 21st century style in Casino Royale, with new Bond star Daniel Craig. Both the car

and Craig are scheduled to make a spectacular return in the upcoming sequel, Quantum of Solace.

Aston Martin dealerships form a central part of the company's image. An award-winning series of modern pavilions in high profile international locations reflect the design and attention to detail offered by the brand's bespoke service. Like its products, the approach does not compromise on materials; the overall look and attention to detail more in keeping with a boutique hotel than a car showroom. Since 2000, CEO Dr Ulrich Bez has overseen a period of growth and investment that ended Aston Martin's 20-year partnership with Ford in June 2007. As an independently owned company its dealership expansion programme has gone from strength-to-strength, with its first two showrooms in China opening in 2008.

Integral to Aston Martin's brand identity is its distinctive winged logo (believed to denote speed) that has evolved over time. Today every car has a hand-made, discreet metal badge on the bonnet and each showroom, a version of the logo rendered in stainless steel and illuminated by LEDs. Inside the cars, the wings are etched onto the sapphire and stainless steel ECU (Emotion Control Unit) inserted into the dashboard to initiate the engine start sequence.

An ability to successfully embrace change, without compromising its worldwide reputation for understated style and elegance, keeps Aston Martin at the pinnacle of car manufacturing; each design combining form, function and material to produce the aesthetic beauty and sporting prowess the brand has been built on.

AVEDA

Embracing the art and science of pure flower and plant essences, Aveda develops, manufactures and markets an extensive collection of plant-based beauty and well-being products; beauty is as beauty does.

aveda.co.uk

When entrepreneur, environmentalist and well-being guru Horst Rechelbacher founded Aveda in 1978, his aim was to provide beauty industry professionals with high performance, botanically-based products that were kind to the skin and the planet.

Rooted in the ancient Eastern principles and practice of Ayurveda – originating in India more than 5,000 years ago and believed to provide the key to well-being – Horst developed Aveda at his home in Minneapolis, using natural plant extracts sourced from around the globe and grown without petrochemical fertilisers, insecticides or herbicides. Thirty years on, Aveda's head office and manufacturing plant are still in Minneapolis and its philosophy remains unchanged: to offer positive choices for living life in balance, with one's self, each other and the Earth.

Of late, Aveda has returned to its Ayurvedic roots with products such as the Chakra™ Balancing Body Mists and the Chakra™ Balancing Massage. Both have been formulated to authentic Ayurvedic chakra balancing traditions, Aveda Chakras™, and are designed to inspire healing, balance and well-being while providing an aromatic journey for mind and body.

But Aveda is about more than just products; it has proved itself to be a trailblazer when it comes to corporate sustainability. While its ingredients are sourced for the least impact to the planet – 90 per cent of the tonnage of essential oils used by Aveda in manufacturing products is certified organic – its focus on packaging and manufacturing, in recent years, has promoted a wave of new initiatives that demonstrate the brand's ongoing environmental commitment.

A high profile example is the Caps Recycling Programme. Launched in September 2008 to mark Aveda's 30th anniversary, it is the first-ever project of its kind in the US, and the thinking behind it – to save marine life by reducing the amount of caps littering the beaches and oceans – reinforces the brand's environmental credentials. The programme debuted with the launch of Aveda's limited edition Vintage Clove Shampoo, an ecological version of its inaugural 1978 product; at 96 per cent, its container boasts the highest percentage of recycled content currently available in the beauty marketplace for this type of coloured plastic.

Another pioneering initiative by Aveda is its adoption of wind power; it is the first beauty company to manufacture with 100 per cent wind power and the brand's funding of new wind energy sources has generated enough energy to offset 100 per cent of the electricity used by its primary manufacturing facility, distribution facility and corporate headquarters in Blaine.

Over the years, Aveda has fostered partnerships with traditional communities in a continued effort to provide more sustainable, natural ingredients. Introducing better traceability to its supply chain has had a positive and significant impact on the indigenous communities it has established connections with, such as the Mardu peoples of Western Australia, the Yawanawa people of the Western Amazon, and the Babassu nut gatherers in north-eastern Brazil.

Aveda products are now available in more than 8,000 salons and spas globally, including many leading salons, spas and department stores in the UK. The colours used in its make-up have been mixed to reflect the vibrancy of nature's palette and while the skin care formulas, in keeping with the brand's mission 'to care for the world we live in', are already plant-packed, the emphasis remains on continually sourcing and developing greener alternatives through ongoing research and developments into plant-derived ingredients.

Aveda's mission is to care for the world; from the products it develops, to the ways in which it gives back to society, Aveda strives to set an example for environmental leadership and responsibility – not just in the world of beauty, but around the world.

BECK'S

A quest for purity and a progressive spirit
is what gives Beck's its distinctive taste
and enduring, authentic appeal.

becks.com

Beck's has been brewed in Bremen, since 1873, in strict accordance with the German purity law 'Reinheitsgebot'. This emphasis on purity lies at the heart of its success.

In 1984 Beck's was launched in the UK, quickly establishing itself as Britain's number one imported lager. Seven million bottles of Beck's are now produced every day to meet global demand.

Throughout the course of its long history Beck's has had only six brew masters, all complying to the strict dictates set by the Reinheitsgebot that guarantee only four natural ingredients – barley-malt, hops, yeast and water – are used for brewing. The regulation (dating back to 1516) produces the crisp, fresh taste Beck's is internationally renowned for and demonstrates the brand's unwavering focus on quality and purity. This attention to detail is also apparent in Beck's Vier – an imported four per cent ABV lager brewed to the same exacting standards as Beck's – and other recent brand extensions such as Alcohol Free and Green Lemon.

Several key inventions have been instrumental in helping the brand's pioneering quest to serve the 'perfect' beer, perhaps the most notable being Carl Linde's cooling machine in 1888, credited with revolutionising the brewing process – until that time beer had been cooled with natural ice during the storage period. This progressive spirit is part of a brand heritage rooted in individualism, from its founder Heinrich Beck to its unerring commitment to Reinheitsgebot – an attribute that the company's advertising and communications celebrate.

The latest campaign by Beck's – rolled out across several mediums – presents a series of modern cultural icons succeeding, not in spite of, but because of their individualism. For instance, the man in a New York hotel room, 'This is the city that said no to sleep' and the 1950s Volkswagen Beetle, 'The car that said no to big' both convey the same message: say no to compromise. The campaign, which signs off with the statement 'different by choice', underlines this by drawing a parallel to Beck's and its uncompromising stance in regard to quality and purity.

Beck's has been sponsoring contemporary art events since 1985 but it was between 1999 and 2007 that it really cemented its active role in the UK's burgeoning art scene when it teamed up with the Institute of Contemporary Arts (ICA) to create Beck's Futures, a competition platform to launch up-and-coming artists. On the back of this it launched Beck's Fusions, further extending the brand's contemporary art credentials by adding music to the mix. A series of unique events, held across the UK, brought together leading musical and artistic talents to create original and inspiring performances; the first, in Trafalgar Square in London, was headlined by The Chemical Brothers. 2008's event is even bigger with the largest scale project of its kind ever undertaken, offering three days of art and music, headlined by Massive Attack in fusion with United Visual Artists.

For the last 20 years Beck's has offered itself up as a canvas to some of the biggest names in contemporary art, such as Damien Hirst and the Chapman Brothers, and in recent years has commemorated major sponsorship deals and exhibition openings by challenging these leading artists to create limited edition bottle labels.

This brand involvement with contemporary culture is continually pushing new boundaries; in 2008, for instance, under the moniker of Beck's Canvas, it forged a new collaboration with the Royal College of Art to offer four promising artists – Riitta Ikonen, Charlotte Bracegirdle, Tom Price and Simon Cunningham – the opportunity to exhibit artwork across 27 million bottles of Beck's; one of the largest ever exhibitions of contemporary art.

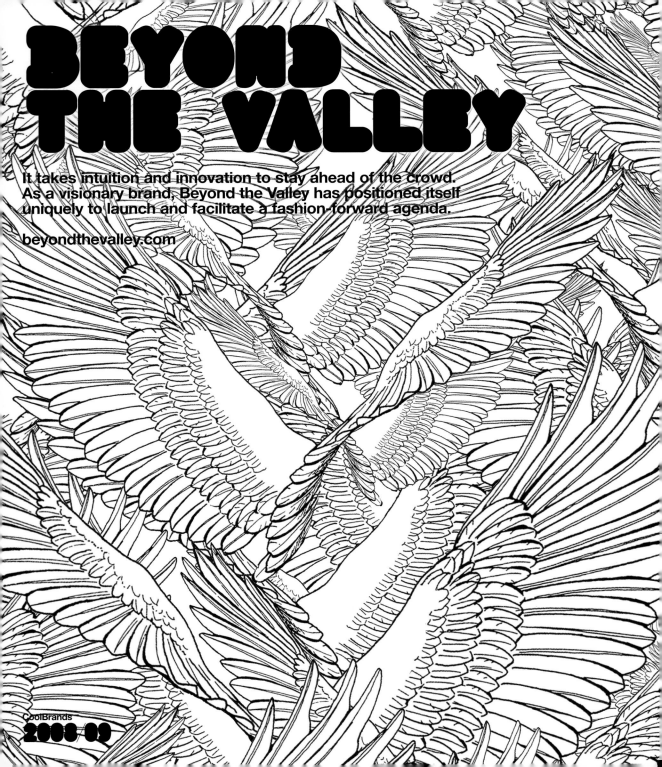

BEYOND THE VALLEY

It takes intuition and innovation to stay ahead of the crowd.
As a visionary brand, Beyond the Valley has positioned itself
uniquely to launch and facilitate a fashion-forward agenda.

beyondthevalley.com

Beyond the Valley

In the four short years since its launch, Beyond the Valley has gone from being a springboard for designers to one of London's leading destinations for fashion innovation and cultural insight.

Beyond the Valley, the brainchild of Jo Jackson, Kate Harwood and Kristjana Williams, moved to its permanent unit in the heart of Soho in 2005. The Newburgh Street concept store – including studio and gallery space – showcases work by cutting-edge global designers; from fashion to wallpaper, fine art to furniture and jewellery to graphic design. But as its name suggests, the brand goes 'beyond' just the shop front; for instance, in its first few years it launched Darkside of the Valley (an exclusive collection for Topshop), crafted a temporary 'guerilla' sister store in Helsinki, and curated Wünderville for the London Design Festival, a multi-venue Victorian 'freakshow' showcasing 15 top designers.

Beyond the Valley's remit continues to expand; it recently launched a limited edition wallpaper range with luxury brand Cole & Son that comprises three distinctive designs using three very different processes. Challenging convention and pushing boundaries is part of the brand's next stage of development. While the store continues to be a mainstay – launching more than 300 designers in the last two years alone – it is only part of the picture. When Beyond the Valley first launched, its aim was to offer eclectic, affordable products from breakthrough talent. Now, after three years of increasing demand for its skill in trend perception and brand consultancy, the concept store has joined

forces with brand experience experts 'i-am' to create a new unit, Beyond the Valley Insight, offering established businesses access to current trends and markets – a unique one-stop package that acquired the burgeoning partnership an impressive list of high profile clients such as Nokia, adidas and Smirnoff, within its first three months alone.

With its propensity for filtering out transient fads, Beyond the Valley's handpicked team (that includes a 100-strong network of talented emerging creatives) is not only able to intuitively spot current trends unfolding in and around the capital's centre but, crucially, apply the relevance of each trend to selected clients, a first-hand rather than passive experience. Working with the proven 'i-am' processes for brand positioning, Beyond the Valley Insight is able to take its clients from initial analysis through to complete,

and non-conventional marketing concepts and final implementation. The role of the concept store remains key in this process by offering a destination for identifying new trends and a test bed for new ideas.

The brand's pioneering credentials were further extended through a series of 'Inverted' experimental environments created for the London Design Festival in September 2008, rolled out in and around the Carnaby area. The main attraction was a pop-up 'Inverted' retail experience – created exclusively for the Festival and open for those two weeks only. A shop of polar opposites, the environment was visually flipped in two, offering brand new fashion and design products in back-to-front and front-to-back versions.

From winning the 'London Young Entrepreneur of the Year' award in 2005, Beyond the Valley has continued in its entrepreneurial bent, taking a pivotal role in London's creative community. Its Autumn/Winter 2008/09 range combines the talents of recent design graduates Jukka Hakkulinen and Colin Henderson, who joined Beyond the Valley to create their first full menswear range for the brand. It will also play host to exclusive fashion collections from AB Irato, Andrea Crews, Ostwald Helgason and Yuko Yoshitake, with new product additions including shoes by Marcello Tochi, accessories and homewares from Christopher Coppens, and ceramics by Bosa for Fabrica.

Photography: Fatsarazzi

BUSABA EATHAI

Conceived by restaurateur Alan Yau, Busaba Eathai is a modern interpretation of the traditional ethnic Thai canteen.

busaba.com

Busaba Eathai (its name derived from a kind of Thai flower and a fusion of the words 'eat' and 'Thai') eschews the restrictions of conventional restaurant dining for a more informal eating experience, based on fast, affordable, healthy food.

Inspired by the social dynamics of sharing dishes around a large communal table, a popular convention in Eastern societies, Yau collaborated with renowned Parisian designer Christian Liaigre – who was also responsible for the interior design in both of his London Michelin-starred restaurants, Hakkasan and Yauatcha – to create and open the Wardour Street Busaba Eathai in 1999. Since then, two further London branches have opened in Store Street and Bird Street – with Busaba Bird Street netting Yau the prestigious 2005 title of 'Independent Restaurateur of the Year' from Caterer Magazine.

In 2008, Busaba Eathai secured substantial investment from Phoenix – whose previous ventures into the casual dining sector include the Gaucho Group and Tootsies – to enable the opening of up to 30 further restaurants across the UK over the next five years.

The informal approach to dining, on which the brand has been built, has gained it a core customer base; one that is happy to queue in time-honoured fashion for a table. Diners rarely have long to wait as the restaurant concept embraces the quick turnaround tradition of Eastern canteens; the average stay per customer is around 45 minutes. Busaba Eathai's decision to shun booking policies is a true reflection of the brand's living ethos, 'sookjai', meaning 'to have pleasure'. Based on Buddhist values, the philosophy encourages people to take a step back from the hectic pace of everyday life.

Featuring warm and tactile materials such as teak, patinated bronze and hewn slate, Liaigre's interior design concept lends itself to this ethos; additional materials used, including bronze, rattan and hardwood, are warmed by the soft lighting from the watercolour paper lampshades. The decoration provides a tranquil backdrop to the dynamics of group eating, structured around sculptured benches and large square tables. Outside, the striking timber and slate frontage incorporates distinctive yet discreete signage, while a menu screen – designed and developed by Tomas Roope at Tomato Interactive – adds an element of interaction and information to the architecture.

Although the menu itself evolves and changes regularly, it always includes an affordable selection of Thai salads, noodles, curries and stir-fries, as well as a takeaway menu with dishes specially packaged in a range of branded containers, designed by Bibliothèque. Chargrilled duck in tamarind sauce is a brand strong-point as is the extensive selection of both hot and cold drinks – which includes unusual combinations such as lemongrass tea with honey – and the range of freshly prepared juices and smoothies. The more unorthodox side dishes, such as Thai calamari with ginger and peppercorns and the prawns with pomelo and coconut wrapped in betel leaves, have become as widely known as the brand itself.

Following the Thai mantra 'gan gin gan yuu' – meaning 'as you eat, so you are' – Busaba Eathai believes that the choice of ingredients, the preparation and presentation are indicative of individual identity. Having hit upon this winning formula, Yau sees little reason to tamper with the brand's shared tables, affordable menu or oriental mystique: a restaurant for those in the know.

CAMBRIDGE AUDIO

As one of the world's leading manufacturers of hi-fi and home cinema equipment, Cambridge Audio's UK-developed products are designed with three key elements in mind: ease-of-use, performance and value for money.

cambridge-audio.com

● Cambridge Audio

For 40 years Cambridge Audio has been at the forefront of the British hi-fi industry, developing some of the most technologically advanced hi-fi, home cinema and multi-room entertainment products on the market.

Founded in 1968, the company went through a number of incarnations before being acquired by Audio Partnership plc in 1994. Since then it has extended its reputation for quality and affordability both in the UK and around the world. Cambridge Audio products are now distributed across 55 countries, turning over in excess of US$40 million.

Cambridge Audio's philosophy is simple: to faithfully recreate music and film through state-of-the-art hi-fi and home cinema products – it's no coincidence that many of the brand's engineers are musicians themselves. Prior to each new product launch, all designs undergo a process of rigorous evaluation and testing that involves meticulous listening and fine tuning.

Landmark products such as the Cambridge Audio 840A – which showcases a new class of amplification (Class XD™) – demonstrate Cambridge Audio's willingness to challenge the status quo where it believes significant improvements can be made. In 2005 it launched Incognito, the world's first truly affordable multi-room package; opening up this exclusive type of product to a far wider audience. It also challenged

the notion (and commonly held industry perception) that such quality necessitates complex operating instructions and prohibitive expense.

One of the reasons attributed to Cambridge Audio's enduring success is the dedication and passion of its workforce. The 80-strong staff, that includes more than 20 engineers working within a dedicated London-based research and development facility, shares its knowledge and enthusiasm for hi-fi and home cinema with a discerning customer base. Unusually for a global brand, Cambridge Audio is a young company with employees typically in their 20s and 30s. Headed up by James Johnson-Flint, founder of Audio Partnership, team cohesion plays a crucial part in brand development and is often facilitated by social events to encourage invention and innovation.

As an early adopter of new media, Cambridge Audio has successfully run promotions and competitions on YouTube; more conventional strategies have centred around developing and implementing creative campaigns across leading hi-fi, home cinema, gadget and technology publications. Its latest offering focuses on the association between people's passion for music and film and the enhancements Cambridge Audio products can offer. To reflect the company's global reach, the campaign has been designed with a universal appeal that transcends cultural boundaries.

As one of the world's most progressive audio equipment manufacturers, integrity is fundamental to the ethos of Cambridge Audio, as demonstrated by an emphasis on ethical and human rights. By only working with partners who share its commitment to protecting and preserving the environment – which includes compliance with local government laws and international standards as well as the US and EU regulations prohibiting the use of ozone-depleting chemicals – Cambridge Audio's pro-active ethical stance ensures all new products adhere to environmental guidelines.

The current Cambridge Audio logo – created in 2002 – updates the original 1968 version with a contemporary 21st century edge. It reflects the company's landmark Azur range that has revolutionised the hi-fi separates market while, at the same time, offering a clean and distinctive brand image the world over.

In 2007 the Azur 840A V2 won Cambridge Audio its first coveted Electronics Image and Sound Association (EISA) award. A panel of EISA judges, comprising journalists from Europe's most respected specialist magazines, voted it two-channel amplifier of the year. With four CES Innovations Awards over the last two years, in recognition of outstanding originality, and a host of gongs from hi-fi and gadget magazines worldwide, Cambridge Audio continues to build on its reputation for unrivalled technology and optimum performance.

CIRQUE DU SOLEIL

Driven by creativity and thriving in the face of a challenge, Cirque du Soleil has proved itself to be as agile and impressive as its world-famous performers.

cirquedusoleil.com

CoolBrands
2008/09

CIRQUE DU SOLEIL.

In 2008, Cirque du Soleil will present 17 shows simultaneously throughout the world. The company has performed to almost 80 million people in more than 200 cities across five continents.

Founded in 1984 with 73 employees, today Cirque du Soleil employs more than 4,000 people, including 1,000 artists performing in shows or training at its International Headquarters in Montreal – a facility housing dance and acrobatics studios, as well as costume and props workshops. The company's ability to adapt, diversify and stay ahead of the curve – by developing unprecedented and original show formats – has ensured its continued success over the years, despite challenging economic conditions. New markets and innovative business and artistic alliances are key elements of its growth strategy.

The 2006 show DELIRIUM, a high-tech multimedia showcase of Cirque du Soleil music, was the first Cirque production to be presented in arena-style venues in North America and Europe. This new tour model allowed the company to bring its shows to locations that were unable to accommodate a big top, giving more people than ever the chance to experience a Cirque du Soleil production. This was followed in 2007 by Wintuk™, at Madison Square Garden, which marked the first time that the company had presented an annual seasonal show produced specifically for the New York market.

Recent years have been prolific for Cirque; the early 2000s saw the company creating an average of one new production every two years. Then in 2008 alone, the curtain rose on a total of three new – and very different – resident shows. Two of them, ZAIA™ in Macau and ZED™ in Tokyo, marked a crucial advance for the company by establishing a permanent presence in Asia. Previously only touring productions had performed on that continent. The third resident show to open in 2008 was CRISS ANGEL® Believe™ in Las Vegas. The creative partnership between acclaimed magician Criss Angel and Cirque du Soleil has produced a breathtaking Las Vegas show that pushes the boundaries of magic and illusion.

Cirque du Soleil's growth and diversification is ongoing: a second show for Macau is already in development, while production is well underway for Cirque's latest touring show to premiere in Montreal in 2009. A movie-themed resident show is also in the pipeline for the Kodak Theatre in Los Angeles, and a production inspired by the life and music of Elvis Presley is due to take up permanent residence in a new theatre at CityCenter in Las Vegas. A further new theatre will open in Dubai to house Cirque's first resident show in the Middle East.

The pioneers of Cirque du Soleil developed a unique mix of different artistic disciplines, combined with acrobatics and circus acts, which gives audiences around the world a contemporary circus show. Since its inception more than a quarter of a century ago, Cirque du Soleil has only ever been satisfied if it is breaking new ground. Today, its biggest challenge is to find ways to manage business growth at a sustainable pace, while offering show creators the possibility to explore new artistic territory.

Cirque du Soleil, Wintuk, ZAIA and ZED are trademarks owned by Cirque du Soleil and used under licence. The trademarks Criss Angel and Believe are owned by Criss Angel and used under licence.

COBRA BEER

**It takes a visionary approach to succeed in being different.
Cobra Beer has a reputation for innovation and a pioneering spirit that
has seen it become one of the fastest growing world beers in the UK.**

cobrabeer.com

PREMIUM BEER
EXTRA SMOOTH

COBRA®
कोबरा

The date: 1989. The place: Bangalore, India. The concept: Cobra, a premium beer specially brewed for added smoothness by Cambridge law graduate, Karan Bilimoria.

But the road to success is not always plain sailing, as Karan discovered when he made plans to export his new brand to the UK; with £20,000 of student debt, no experience and a recession looming it was the start of an interesting journey.

Fast-forward 19 years. Cobra has come a long way from being sold door-to-door to London's Indian restaurants from the back of Karan's battered Citroen 2CV. Since this early hand-to-mouth existence, growth has skyrocketed – the brand now sells in 50 countries worldwide with annual sales of £126 million in 2006/07.

Karan's dissatisfaction with the range of beers being served in Indian restaurants, which he perceived to be too fizzy and bland to complement the food, lies behind Cobra. Karan's idea was to create a beer with the refreshing qualities of lager, but the smoothness and fuller flavour of ale.

While the original premium beer was itself a success, having less gas than regular lagers, over the past few years Cobra has continued to innovate, adding four new products to its portfolio. Cobra Zero% alcohol-free and Cobra Light came first, followed by King Cobra – the world's first double-fermented lager – which, befitting such a special bottle-conditioned beer, comes packaged in elegant Champagne-style bottles. The brand's latest product, Cobra Bite, is an exotic range of flavoured premium lagers with 100 per cent natural extracts, including blood orange, sweet lime and lemongrass.

The quality of Cobra products consistently sets it apart from other beers, accruing considerable industry recognition and kudos along the way. At the prestigious Monde Selection Awards, for instance, Cobra has been awarded gold medals every year since 2001.

Cobra has developed its film presence by becoming the official Beer of the British Film Institute (BFI) and its festivals, including The Times BFI London Film Festival, and has also launched a year-long sponsorship of the Curzon Group, covering seven cinemas across the UK. In 2007, Cobra was the fastest growing world beer in the UK in both the on- and off-trade markets. The brand's profile looks set to increase further thanks to its biggest-ever marketing campaign, designed to launch Cobra firmly into the mainstream. The integrated £14 million 'Now you're talking' campaign includes an £8.4 million multi-media spend across television, cinema, press, outdoor advertising and online

as well as a £2.1 million, year-long sponsorship of the TV channel Dave.

A re-working of Cobra's branding and packaging will be backed up by a nationwide sampling campaign featuring replica AC Cobra racecars and events including Taste of London, the Henley Regatta and the Goodwood Festival of Speed.

In 2005, Cobra established the Cobra Foundation, an independent charity that gives money to groups working to improve the lives of children

in India and the UK. The Cobra Foundation embodies Cobra's commitment to giving back to the community – a pledge dating back to its earliest days, when Cobra donated beer to community groups and charities for fundraisers and events.

When Karan Bilimoria poured his first Cobra in Bangalore, back in 1989, the odds were stacked against him. But he had a mission: to brew the finest Indian beer and make it a global brand. Karan can raise his glass to that.

CREATIVE REVIEW

As the voice of critique for the creative industries, Creative Review is constantly seeking new ways through which to communicate. When it speaks, its audience will want to listen.

creativereview.co.uk

CoolBrands
2008/09

Creative Review is the UK's leading title for creatives working in advertising and design, and for anyone who has an interest in innovative, new and stylish work in the area.

Starting life 28 years ago, Creative Review has grown from being just a print magazine into a much larger brand, incorporating online blogs, events, awards, conferences and exhibitions, as well as the monthly title. Regardless of the media format, the aim remains the same – to present the best new creative work from around the world, from the most exciting new talent to the most important new trends in graphic design, advertising, new media, photography, illustration, typography and beyond. During its lifetime, Creative Review has become a respected authority on all aspects of creativity and the magazine is now read in more than 82 countries worldwide.

Its experience in the field makes Creative Review well placed to run several award schemes throughout the year, such as the Annual series. Selected in collaboration with a panel of leading industry figures, the Annual is a showcase for the best and most significant work of the year in visual communications, encompassing advertising, graphic design, digital media,

packaging, music videos and related media. The Photography Annual celebrates work across categories ranging from advertising to editorial and conceptual photography.

Guided by the 'practice what you preach' philosophy, Creative Review believes the look and feel of the magazine itself to be as important as the work featuring within its pages; the innovative and stylish editorial design has been recognised by both the Art Directors Club (ADC) and the D&AD. The simple logo, 'CR' set within a solid square, is an instantly recognisable brand stamp that, coupled with striking cover visuals, ensures Creative Review is a magazine with shelf presence in the newsagents

and book stores through which it is distributed.

As the voice that critiques creativity, the brand cannot afford to fall behind the creative pack. Through actively exploring new forms of media and brand communications, Creative Review remains at the leading-edge of the market, continuing to make contact with clients and customers in innovative and interesting ways. 'Virtual Bios Teasers' is a core example: a patented communications art, it allows elements of motion, imagery, audio and conversation to be injected into a short viral clip, which can then be sent or displayed instantly on multiple platforms. The technique sums up the Creative Review tactic to never send a word when

an image can be sent instead and to never send something static when it can be brought to life. Its extensive and ever-growing archive of content is also put to work, used in motion-based files for mobile phones and MP4 playback.

The need to remain innovative in its communications, exploiting new technologies, is not viewed as an invitation or an excuse to lose the personal touch. Creative Review's communications are carefully targeted towards intended recipients, ensuring maximum impact, while building its reputation as a brand with a voice that readers, brand associates and partners will want to listen to.

DAZED & CONFUSED

Breaking with convention is one thing; Dazed & Confused goes further, pushing boundaries to achieve unrivalled visual and editorial content in a quest to showcase headline-grabbing events.

dazeddigital.com

CoolBrands
2008/09

DAZED & CONFUSED

With its agenda-setting editorial, world-beating fashion, renowned photography and striking illustration, Dazed & Confused has come a long way since its launch in the early 1990s.

Dazed & Confused, now distributed in more than 40 countries and with admirers and imitators across the globe, above all else, prides itself on its independence – a rare phenomenon in magazine publishing.

Founded by prodigious photographer Rankin, and writer and cultural enthusiast Jefferson Hack – and taking its name (as well as its freewheeling spirit) from the classic Led Zeppelin song – Dazed & Confused started out as a limited-run fold-out poster back in 1992. Early cover stars, helping to establish its credentials, included PJ Harvey, Damien Hirst, Richard Ashcroft, Chloe Sevigny, Jarvis Cocker, Robert Carlyle, Kate Moss and Milla Jovovich. It was during this time that Dazed cemented its growing international reputation for daring; extending its editorial remit beyond fashion, music and film, not only taking on the cultural stalwarts of art and literature but tackling both local and international social and political themes, a gambit that instantly marked it out from other glossies.

CLOUDED IN TULLE, REGAL TONES AND POLKA DOT COCKTAIL DRESSES, THIS ECCENTRIC DEBUTANTE

PHOTOGRAPHY JOSH OLINS
STYLING JOANNA SCHLENZKA

RULES THE MANOR, SEDUCING SUITORS WITH HER SIGNATURE LOOK OF PEARLS, FEATHER BOAS AND OPERA GLOVES

Once its fashion, photography and art content became recognised as amongst the best in the world, Dazed set about bringing its music and film editorial up to similar standards by featuring a long list of UK and world firsts, including the likes of Eminem, The Libertines, Pharrell Williams and Alicia Keys. More recently, cover exclusives have included The White Stripes, Maggie Gyllenhaal, Bloc Party, Zooey Deschanel, Sofia Coppola, Justin Timberlake, the Yeah Yeah Yeahs and Selma Blair.

The brand's online offering, DazedDigital.com, now in its second year, extends its trademark cutting-edge and groundbreaking ethos to a wider audience via the web. The world's first Ideas Sharing Network, DazedDigital.com posts exclusive video interviews, live footage of tomorrow's music stars, behind-the-scenes fashion reports, and exclusive features above and beyond what appears in the magazine. Daily blogs and submissions

from its extended global network of accomplished writers, photographers, artists and activists ensure that the brand remains at the forefront of cultural change. Dazed has also taken its long established tradition of nurturing and supporting new talent to the next level in the Rise section of DazedDigital.com, where new talent in music, illustration, fashion and photography is profiled by Dazed's in-house creatives.

The magazine's strong music association has seen the Dazed & Confused brand rolled out to high profile live concerts, such as 2007's War Child benefit at the London club Koko, which featured upcoming stars the Noisettes, Metronomy, Friendly Fires and Late of the Pier.

Today, still 100 per cent independent in ownership and spirit, Dazed & Confused rates as one of the most influential monthly magazines in the world. Recent international launches such as Dazed Korea in 2008 – which sold 80,000 copies in its first month – and Dazed Japan, launched in 2002 and boasting a significant fan base, reinforce its global status.

But far from resting on its reputation, DazedDigital.com is now pushing its taste and influence into new areas, bringing the brand to life in more ways than ever, and engaging a new generation of switched-on, intelligent, aware and influential individuals.

DECLÉOR

As the original and pioneering expert in aromatherapy skin care, Decléor continues to push the boundaries, revolutionising the use of essential oils to deliver the best in service, treatments and products.

decleor.co.uk

CoolBrands

2008 09

The therapeutic powers of aromatherapy are Decléor's passion. More than 35 years of dedicated research into the plant world underlies its carefully developed collection of products and treatments, caring for every aspect of the face and body.

As a brand Decléor focuses on rebalancing the mind, body and spirit, treating not just physical symptoms but every aspect of people's day-to-day lives. Decléor's range of products and treatments are not only beneficial for soothing, healing and moisturising but can also stimulate the olfactory senses, influencing the way the body feels.

Research and innovation play an important role at Decléor. International research laboratories based in France, Japan and the US provide specialist insight into the benefits of essential oils on the skin and psyche; skin knowledge is translated into the brand's comprehensive range of aromatherapy and phytotherapy products. Uniting science with nature enables the development of increasingly effective cosmetic formulas, all of which adhere to a guiding principle: to respect both the environment and an individual's natural beauty.

Over the years, aromatherapy has proved itself to be a tangible science that uses the most active extracts of aromatic plants, the essential oils, to create effective skin care solutions. Essential oils have many properties, and once expertly blended can help to regulate each of the skin's basic functions: hydration, sebum excretion, stimulating cell renewal and defending against internal or external aggressors. Decléor ensures that only the purest essential oils are used in its Aromessences™, each sourced from quality producers worldwide – guaranteeing quality and effective results time-after-time.

The key to the brand's success lies in the Aromessence™, a powerful cocktail of essential oil concentrates that are 100 per cent pure, natural, active and preservative-free. Each of these carefully blended aromatic essences, developed for use on either face or body, has a natural affinity with the skin and penetrates easily and deeply where it is dispersed, leaving no oily residue.

Decléor's entire beauty philosophy is based on a simple yet effective two-fold system called the 'Aroma-Duo Concept', in which the Aromessences™ play a key role; that of acting as a natural beauty 'booster' when used in conjunction with a phytotherapy product. Each Aromessence™ and phytotherapy product is developed to correspond to a particular skin care 'prescription', achieving optimum results on all skin types; it

is proven that using the duo concept dramatically improves results on both the face and body by up to 33 per cent.

Decléor's professional roots have long been associated with luxurious but highly effective treatments – designed to work in harmony with today's lifestyles, whilst ensuring that all skin types are provided with tailor made treatments to suit the individual. Starting with massage techniques that centre around the nervous system and meridians, every Decléor treatment begins with a unique back diagnostic massage where a trained specialist uses pure Aromessences™ to aid drainage and promote a deep sense of relaxation. This diagnostic massage also enables the therapist to assess a client's general condition and skin health in order to select the correct Aromessences™ and professional concentrates for treatment. Each individual treatment – from facials to slimming, firming and relaxation – reinforces the Decléor philosophy of treating a person as a 'whole'.

Decléor is recognised around the world as the trusted expert and innovator in premium aromatherapy skin care, providing luxurious aromatherapy products and treatments for the face and body – revealing the pure essence of nature.

DE'LONGHI

Innovation is the life-blood of De'Longhi, along with a commitment to quality and style that has kept it at the forefront of contemporary design for more than 100 years.

delonghi.co.uk

De'Longhi's heritage is firmly rooted in domestic appliances: the family-run business, which evolved from a craftsman's workshop into a small appliance company in the 1950s, had launched its first range of branded goods by the 1970s – portable electric radiators.

In the kitchen, De'Longhi revolutionised the marketplace with the launch of products such as the Rotofryer – a deep fryer with a rotating basket and patented oil drain hose – and the Bean-to-cup Magnifica, Perfecta and PrimaDonna coffee maker ranges, complete with patented 'single touch' espresso and cappuccino functions. Each range fuelled organic growth in new areas, eventually driving further diversification of the brand through notable acquisitions such as Simac Vetrella in 1989, and Kenwood in 2001.

De'Longhi's success is embedded in its definitive style that renders products instantly recognisable. 2008 saw the brand build on increasing its market share of the coffee sector with the launch of two new Perfecta Bean-to-cup coffee machines. It also rolled out a distinctive and contemporary range of kettles and toasters, Icona, that featured heavily in the style pages of ES Magazine, the Daily Mail, Ideal Homes, the FT and House Beautiful, amongst others, thanks to a unique high gloss, three-layer paint finish, unrivalled by other brands.

Recent brand promotional activity has been strongly linked to De'Longhi's new coffee-centric approach; a monthly magazine column, a specialist online coffee site – www.seriousaboutcoffee.com – and an eight-page booklet (dedicated purely to De'Longhi coffee) are ongoing campaigns while its most widely publicised and extravagant strategy to date, 'Caffe Raro', saw it join forces with coffee expert and Barista champion David Cooper, to create the world's most expensive

coffee. The limited edition blend of Jamaican Blue Mountain beans and rare Kopi Luwak, topped with a sprinkling of gold leaf, received widespread press coverage when it was sold exclusively at Peter Jones department store in Sloane Square.

De'Longhi applies the same creativity to its fundraising activities as it does to its products; in 2007, an auction featuring bespoke coffee-themed works of art – donated by renowned artists such as Damien Hirst – raised funds of more than £90,000 for Macmillan Cancer Support.

Unique and unconventional: De'Longhi's philosophy is based on delivering the best in terms of style, performance, efficiency and quality. In order to facilitate the brand's competitive edge and maintain its market position, it invests in state-of-the-art research and design facilities, while through pitching itself as a 'helpful' brand it continues to field resources into help-at-hand guides, product helplines and increased website accessibility.

Awards won by De'Longhi reinforce the brand's core values. For example, recognition for 'stand innovation' at consumer exhibitions such as the Good Food Show, at Birmingham's NEC – where a four metre high Argento toaster was featured at its hub.

Owner and founder of the De'Longhi Group, Giuseppe De'Longhi, is very much at the core of the organisation; from major acquisitions through to product design and marketing. His son Fabio, the Group CEO, is similarly involved across most facets of the business. It's frequently said that were you to cut a De'Longhi employee in half they would be blue and white (like the logo)… a testament to the brand. From the top down, De'Longhi engenders loyalty and enthusiasm in its employees; a definitive pride in the brand.

Be it products, marketing or simply making domestic life easier, De'Longhi is a brand driven by innovation and a focus on its customers' quality of life. Through continued development, investment and seminal design it has its sights set clearly and firmly on the future.

DERMALOGICA

Play. Learn. Shop. Words not usually associated with skin care, but then Dermalogica is no ordinary skin care company.

dermalogica.co.uk

dermalogica®
a skin care system researched and developed by The International Dermal Institute

A holistic and educational approach to skin therapy has cemented Dermalogica's reputation as a forward-thinking brand with universal appeal – no mean feat in today's highly competitive skin care industry.

Since 1983 it has set about quietly revolutionising skin care through a unique synthesis of science, non-toxic ingredients and traditional philosophies. When Jane and Raymond Wurwand founded The International Dermal Institute, their mission was simple: to provide a training facility for professional skin therapists and initiate an industry standard for the skin care profession.

It was just the beginning. Rejecting existing market products as unsuitable – due to the irritants used that caused adverse reactions – Jane set about creating a skin therapy system based on her ethos of health and well-being, rather than manufactured beauty. Dermalogica's aim was to harness science and nature to devise innovative and effective formulations and treatments; banning known irritants from products was key to the brand's philosophy.

To this day International Dermal Institute Training Centres worldwide are still used to research and develop all Dermalogica products, elevating the quality of education to an unprecedented level and providing a unique forum where skin care professionals can trade experiences and ideas. The brand takes a non-compromising stance in support of therapists, through a series of bold trade advertisements, with the predominant strapline, 'It's my industry and I'm taking it back', reasserting its standing as a champion of the skin care professional.

What continues to set Dermalogica apart from its competitors is its emphasis on innovation, education and information. 2008 marked the launch of three new products, reinforcing this progressive stance: Age Smart™, challenging the notion behind many anti-ageing remedies – that visible signs of ageing should be masked – by addressing biochemical reactions that trigger physical changes before they occur; MediBac Clearing™, a 24-hour treatment designed to combat the increasingly common (and embarrassing) condition of adult acne; and Shave, a range of skin care solutions for men, designed with speed and dual-purpose applications in mind.

Radical product development keeps Dermalogica firmly ensconced in the pages of leading style titles such as Elle and Marie Claire and adds ever-more industry and consumer awards to its burgeoning trophy cabinet. 2008 saw it secure four more wins at the InStyle Best Beauty Buy Awards and 11 Natural Health Beauty Awards for Product Excellence. Daily Microfoliant, meanwhile, topped the More! readers' Ultimate Beauty Wishlist and was named as the leading product in 2008's 50 Best Beauty Buys list. Further wins and nominations came by way of You and Your Wedding, Bridal Beauty Awards and The Independent's 50 Best Men's Grooming Products. Given the company's non-reliance on consumer advertising its success is all the more notable. Promotion is largely confined to press coverage and word-of-mouth recommendations; a refreshing marketing approach that has established enviable industry credentials and a cult following amongst top make-up artists and celebrities.

Today Dermalogica embraces its 'best-kept secret' role with celebrity endorsements both in the UK and the US.

As part of its ongoing mission to introduce increasingly diverse education, the flagship Dermalogica stores in London and Berlin offer customers free education via fun, interactive classes, designed to fulfil their desire to learn more about skin and to experience the Dermalogica brand hands-on.

The core values of innovation, function and education remain integral to the Dermalogica brand identity. However, a brand's commitment to its foundations doesn't imply inertia. On the contrary, success depends on progression and momentum – evolving whilst maintaining credibility. Dermalogica's research background enables it to anticipate industry trends and maintain its key position at the forefront of new developments in skin therapy.

DISARONNO

Disaronno's sense of effortless, sociable style and Italian chic make it an ideal liqueur for any occasion.

disaronno.co.uk

CoolBrands
2008/09

DISARONNO

Think of Italy, think of romance. The warm, sophisticated taste of Disaronno has a lineage dating back to one of the most romantic periods in Italian history – the Renaissance.

In 1525, the artist Bernardino Luini – a student of the Leonardo Da Vinci School of Art – was commissioned to paint a fresco of the Madonna in Saronno, Italy. Legend has it that Bernardino and his muse (a beautiful innkeeper) fell deeply in love – culminating in the young widow creating a sweet tasting liqueur in honour of her lover. This gift was the first bottle of Disaronno; its name derived from the phrase 'di Saronno' – meaning of, or from, Saronno.

It was Domenico Reina who created the Disaronno 'Originale' recipe, based on the innkeeper's elixir, towards the end of the 18th century.

The secret blend of herbs and fruits, steeped in apricot kernel oil, has been a closely guarded Reina family secret ever since.

As well as its unmistakeable flavour of marzipan and honey – unchanged since 1525 – Disaronno is also known for its distinctively shaped bottle. The first bottle, classic and elaborate, was heavily influenced by Renaissance style. Over the years it has evolved gradually into its current squarer form, with the stopper becoming a recognisable trademark. The current bottle was realised in the 1970s by a master craftsman from Murano: its unique square shape and bevelled, hand-crafted glass design is now recognised as a modern classic.

Brand marketing activity strongly focuses on the sophisticated Italian chic long associated with Disaronno. Television has been an important medium in conveying this style and sophistication to a wider audience. Set in an elegant bar, its most recent campaign, 'Pass the Pleasure Around', concentrates on the taste of Disaronno –

one 'that makes you wish it will never end'.

Disaronno has a long history of collaborating with influential designers with a passion for cutting-edge glamour, for example its sponsorship of Vivienne Westwood's Red Label London Fashion Week show in February 2008. Such high profile fashion associations fit well with the development of bespoke brand activity. Disaronno regularly brings together fashion and lifestyle experts to provide style tips and advice, with targeted activity such as 2008's 'Disaronno Style Squad' – fronted by leading stylist Nicky Hambleton-Jones, celebrity hairstylist Richard Ward and fashion and lifestyle expert Nick Ede – proving to be an effective way of heightening brand awareness amongst stylish young women.

Alongside this, Disaronno recognises that it is taste that counts, which is why sampling and promotions at key times and in a variety of locations also play an important role within the brand's marketing plan.

Created as a demonstration of love during the Renaissance, Disaronno uses Valentine's Day, and the month of February every year, to raise awareness and promote trial. 'With Love', 2008's offering, encouraged consumers to try a Disaronno cocktail in order to receive a gift of free chocolates. In summertime, meanwhile, promotions such as 'Pitcher Perfect' offer the opportunity to experience Disaronno in refreshing and modern long drinks. Whatever the season, Disaronno's taste and versatility continues to strengthen its reputation as an indispensable cocktail ingredient and perennial favourite of the sophisticated set.

From timeless cocktails to coffee, or simply 'over ice', Disaronno is an enduring legacy of the Renaissance and the Italian belief in love and style.

FALKE

FALKE products are the result of innovative development; fashionable clothing made from premium materials, manufactured with the finest workmanship and characterised by the brand's high functionality.

falke.com

CoolBrands
2008/09

F A L K E

In 1895, Franz Falke-Rohen set up a small knitting company in Germany. Today, FALKE is a global brand with more than 199 franchises – 138 national and 61 international – and is managed by the fourth Falke generation, Franz-Peter and Paul Falke.

FALKE's international expansion began in the early 1970s with the opening of production units in South Africa, Portugal and Hungary. It was further reinforced during the 1980s when the brand began working closely with international designers such as Armani, and became licensed partners with Boss, JOOP! and Kenzo, developing, producing and distributing knitted socks and hosiery – in addition to knitwear.

The continued globalisation of the FALKE brand remains a key brand strategy, bolstered by new shops and showrooms abroad and the systematic expansion of sales and marketing organisations in Europe and America. What continues to set FALKE apart from other textile and clothing companies is its commitment to retaining a high proportion of its workforce in Germany; the percentage of staff employed in the Group's home country is virtually identical to the total number of staff it employs abroad.

The distinctive style of the FALKE brand is typified by its flagship Berlin store, which opened in April 2006 and is listed as one of the world's 'best-designed flagship stores' in a book published by specialist architecture and design trade publishers, Avedition. The successful 'shop-in-shop' concept was further developed and has been implemented at leading retailers in key international locations since.

It is the desirability of the FALKE umbrella brand that drives its growth strategy. Three distinct business sectors – legwear, sportswear and knitwear – have helped to establish and maintain its market dominance through a combination of innovation and sophisticated design. A recent strategic step to further enhance its portfolio was the purchase of the Burlington brand in April 2008, which will remain as an independent trademark within the FALKE Group.

The brand's design innovation has also been recognised over the years through a host of awards; from the German Environmental Prize in 1994 – for the development of Clima Wool, an environmentally friendly and insulating material made of wool – to the Design Award of the Federal Republic of Germany in 2007, for a seamless high-tech sports pullover from the FALKE Ergonomic Sport System range. In 2008 the brand also introduced

its own prize, reinforcing the brand's commitment to fostering new and creative textile talent; the FALKE Design Award 2008 was presented to the University of Arts Berlin in recognition of the faculty's work with the manufacturer.

FALKE was an early advocate of the importance of combining function with fashion in the clothing industry, identifying the trend and incorporating it into its brand philosophy: to create intelligent, practical products that are, at the same time, aesthetically pleasing. Over the years the FALKE brand has established itself as an integral part of the fashion market and continues to design and manufacture stylish accessories that meet consumers' individual lifestyles and requirements.

FEVER-TREE

Fever-Tree's range of premium natural mixers has reinvigorated the drinks category, changing perceptions of the importance of the mixer and putting gin & tonic firmly back on the cocktail circuit.

fever-tree.com

PREMIUM   MIXERS

NATURAL

FEVER-TREE

Only the finest natural ingredients

The question posed by Charles Rolls and Tim Warrillow was simple: why craft premium spirits and then compromise the experience by masking the flavour with poor quality mixers?

Following a 'tonic tasting' in 2000 to find the best on the US market, Rolls – who had built his reputation running Plymouth Gin – joined forces with Warrillow, who had a background in luxury food marketing, to analyse the composition of mixers. The pair discovered that the majority of mixers were preserved with sodium benzoate or similar substances, while the use of cheap lemon aromatics (like decanal) and artificial sweeteners (such as saccharin) was widespread – a combination that was affecting the tasting experience and driving customers away from the sector.

So, in 2004, they began creating mixers using natural and fresh ingredients. Fever-Tree Premium Indian Tonic Water launched in the UK in early 2005, the brand name chosen due to 'Fever Tree' being the colloquial name for the Cinchona Tree in which quinine, a key ingredient for tonic, is found. The highest quality quinine was sourced from the Rwanda Congo border and blended with spring water

and eight botanical flavours, including rare ingredients such as marigold extracts and a bitter orange from Tanzania. Crucially, no artificial sweeteners, preservatives or flavourings were added.

The highly carbonated tonic, consisting of small 'champagne' bubbles for a smoother taste, was packaged in 200ml single-serve glass bottles, the perfect size for a double measure gin & tonic; the glass packaging was designed to reflect the premium natural values of the brand and to ensure freshness.

Without a proper marketing budget the company's future lay in the hands of editorial exposure. A short piece in the national press in the summer

of 2005 elicited an instant and positive response. Sales rose dramatically and Waitrose, looking to revamp its mixer category, approached the company to list the product. One month later it was on shelf and Waitrose's share of the mixer market grew from seven to eight per cent in just one year. Majestic, Oddbins, Harrods, Harvey Nichols, Selfridges and Fortnum & Mason also started selling Fever-Tree, subsequently followed by Sainsbury's and Tesco in 2008. During this period of success, the Fever-Tree mixer range blossomed to include an award-winning Bitter Lemon, Ginger Ale (using three natural gingers from Cochin, Ecuador and Nigeria) and the world's first all-natural lower calorie tonic water.

Leading bartenders quickly cottoned on to the benefits of a great mixer; today, Fever-Tree's premium mixers are available in more than 500 high quality establishments countrywide. Internationally, it can be found in six out of the top 10 restaurants in the world (as voted for by Restaurant magazine in 2008). In Spain, the world's largest premium gin & tonic market per capita, Fever-Tree Premium Indian Tonic Water has been immortalised at El Bulli, where world-renowned chef Ferran Adria turned it into a course in itself: 'Sopa de Fever-Tree tonica'. In the US, the world's largest mixers market, Fever-Tree was awarded 'Best New Product' at the 2008 Tales of the Cocktail awards.

The most powerful endorsements, however, have come from the trade; there is universal support of Fever-Tree's reinvigoration of the long overlooked mixer sector, a David and Goliath battle against the conglomerate power of the mass market brands. Spirit companies have also been quick to endorse the brand and the Fever-Tree team now work on sampling and co-promotion opportunities with many of the premium companies such as Belvedere, Tanqueray, Bombay Sapphire, Johnnie Walker and Plymouth Gin, driving Rolls and Warrillow's ambition of quality mixers being drunk by every quality conscious imbiber. After all, if three quarters of your long drink is the mixer, then that mixer should be good.

FIRST DIRECT

With its distinctive monochrome livery and innovative 'unbank' positioning, first direct is challenging convention and putting the 'black and white' back into banking.

firstdirect.com

No
scripts

No
machines

dir

st direc

first direct

first direct

first direct

Launched in 1989, first direct offered an alternative to traditional banking; connecting its customers to real people, it was the first 24-hour, 365-day telephone bank in the UK.

Its refreshing approach to customer service, along with market leading Internet Banking and Mobile Banking propositions, ensured first direct topped the tables in both customer satisfaction and recommendation (Source: NOP 1992) – while collecting an array of awards to boot. As time moved on, its recipe for success was emulated by competitors; anti-bank positioning reappeared as a communications tool, while telephone and internet have since become the banking norms.

Faced with an increasingly competitive environment, first direct set out to recapture the original idea from which the brand was born. Research identified its founding principle of customer service – provided by real people in the UK, all day, every day – to be as relevant as ever. It also came as no surprise that customers were looking for a bank that was 'fair and transparent': first direct was going to have to go back to its 'black and white' roots in every way.

Positioning customers at the heart of the brand strategy – building on the 'machines don't care' tenet embedded within the first direct culture – a new range of banking and savings products was launched in November 2007. Customer communications saw a return to clean, simple, black and white typography as well as high quality print materials, which incorporate a hint of silver embossing; a premium feel intended to reflect valued custom. From the brand itself,

to the first direct interactive website, the Internet Banking portal and direct mail, all were redesigned, breathing the 'black and white' back into the bank.

Secure in its customer service credentials, first direct made a clear statement of confidence by introducing a service guarantee. Alongside the existing £100 joining incentive, should new customers be dissatisfied with the service after six months, they're able to move banks and receive a further £100 from the service guarantee, under the banner of '£100 if you like us, £200 if you don't'.

More than eighteen years after challenging convention by introducing 24-hour banking every day of the year, first direct remains driven by innovation, being the first to offer a seamless online experience for all iPhone and iPod Touch users. It has also extended its 'human touch' to the web, building on its interactive

website with features including podcasts and up-to-date information on the brand and its products, as well as topical commentary on a whole range of issues, from energy saving tips to showcasing the first direct-sponsored 50 Women of Substance exhibition.

The site also includes a 'virtual forest', encouraging customers to log in to their internet banking and opt out of receiving paper statements. For each customer who does this, first direct plants one tree in the virtual forest. For every 20 trees, a real tree will be planted. Visitors can watch the virtual forest grow, and vote for where the real trees should be located – current sites include Bristol, Leeds, London, Manchester and the Midlands. In 2007, 3,500 real trees were planted, while the target for the end of December 2008 – to exceed 6,000 trees – took just six months to achieve.

'Black and white' to the core of its communications, products and services, first direct stands for transparency and fairness in the banking marketplace; the bank for people who don't like banking.

Satisfaction guaranteed

G-STAR RAW

G-Star Raw is luxury streetwear; the introduction of the Raw Denim concept in 1996 reinforced the unorthodox creativity on which the brand has established its credentials and revolutionised the denim industry.

g-star.com

G-Star Raw pushes boundaries. Since its inception in Amsterdam, in 1989, exploration and continuous product development have remained core brand principles. Its timeless style transcends generations while eccentric combinations deliver authenticity.

From its distribution roots in the Benelux, G-Star expanded rapidly in the early 1990s, both in its range and market potential; a collaboration with French designer Pierre Morisset added a new approach to G-Star's product design. Today, G-Star Raw has become a permanent fixture in the denim market across the globe. Recognised for its architectural styles, G-Star's wide reaching appeal – it now distributes to retail outlets in 70 countries – has emerged from its challenging combination of 'street' with 'luxury'.

The company's fundamental aim – to express its passion for denim – has been translated into a store concept by G-Star's own interior design team. Featuring in more than 120 G-Star stores, raw materials such as wood, leather, concrete and steel are key in representing the identity and characteristics of the brand in a tangible form. G-Star's philosophy and market approach – 'just the product' – is deceptively simple. Setting the standards of innovation in denim, G-Star continually explores the material's potential; from unconventional designs and highly luxurious styles to complicated treatment techniques, sustainable alternatives and detailed embellishments.

The Spring/Summer 2009 collection brings new cuts and creations to the catwalk, with craftsmanship at its core: revolutionary pattern construction sees the corkscrew-inspired Arc Pant introduced, lightweight denim increases consumer choice, while coated fabrics and vintage washes sit alongside rubberised and unexpected detailing.

Collection highlights include the NY Raw Special Edition, incorporating fine wools and silks, the Midnight Program – classic formal wear, with a G-Star 'raw luxury' twist – and the astronaut-inspired Space Nomad trouser style, designed to be the ultimate in high-tech comfort.

The introduction of Correct Line adds further interest to G-Star's offering. This range of tailored styles for men and women uses cashmere, silk, leather and cotton materials, blending with denim in all of its forms.

The G-Star brand, meanwhile, is kept in the spotlight through a significant presence at high profile events, such as New York Fashion Week and Tokyo Designer's Week. All brand activities, whether media campaigns, the G-Star fashion shows or collection presentations to the industry, are infused with the company's core values: raw, pure, original, uncooked and unexpected.

G-Star Raw Nights exemplify these values and show G-Star to be a brand keen to create a dialogue with its worldwide following. The series was developed as an entertainment platform and challenges artists to experiment with audience interaction, in orchestrated situations in nightclubs, galleries or even car-parks.

Other brand extensions, such as the Raw Crossover concept, have been instrumental in raising G-Star's profile while underlining its philosophy. Following the launch of Raw Defender and the Raw Ferry, G-Star has joined forces with expert American bike maker, Cannondale, to produce the Raw Cannondale: a pared-down machine stripped back to the bare essentials. The result, launched in 2008, is a premium bike that combines quality and functionality with clean aesthetics and subtle design – key components of the G-Star Raw brand.

Over the course of its history, G-Star's groundbreaking products have been formally recognised by the fashion industry; a host of awards, the Dutch 'Grand Seigneur' and 'Best Denim' SIFA to name just two, have fuelled G-Star's ambition to lead the way in denim innovation.

GAGGIA

Grounded in quality, innovation and tradition, Gaggia's passion for producing the perfect cup of coffee has placed it firmly at the heart of café culture.

gaggia.uk.com

GAGGIA®

Modern coffee-making methods owe much to Achille Gaggia. In 1938 he patented the first modern machine and in doing so, revolutionised the way that coffee was made.

Before this landmark invention, espresso relied on blasting coffee grounds with steam, but Gaggia's ingenious design forced water to flow over the grounds at high pressure, producing the 'crema' unique to espresso. Since the company was founded in 1947, Gaggia has continued to build on this early innovation and is renowned for making consistently high quality machines. Widely acknowledged as a leading authority within the industry, its distinctive red and white logo is associated globally with authentic Italian coffee.

Gaggia machines not only grace coffee shops and restaurants around the world, but also bring a little bit of Italy into the home. It was during the 1970s – a time when bar quality espresso was growing in popularity – that Gaggia produced its first domestic machine. The Baby Gaggia helped to propel the brand to the forefront of the domestic machine market, a position it has retained since, despite robust competition. To celebrate 30 years of the Baby, Gaggia introduced five new versions of the machine in 2007. The range includes a variety of colours, finishes and features all based around the original model.

Gaggia prides itself on the use of cutting-edge technology combined with traditional design. By allowing its design and performance to speak for itself, Gaggia has created an understated, yet highly effective, marketing strategy. Coffee, like many commodities today, now comes in various manifestations to cater for a wide diversity of tastes, from beans and ground form to pods and capsules. As such, this demands a wider variety of coffee machines. Gaggia is the only brand to manufacture machines in three categories – Traditional, Bean-to-cup and Capsules – for both professional and home markets.

Following the introduction of the new Baby range, Gaggia launched further products in the traditional sector, introducing stainless steel boilers to the machines. Designed to be more energy efficient but without compromising on the quality of the coffee, the same principle also underlies the new professional Deco range.

2007 also gave rise to a new generation of automatic machines, capable of producing Italian espresso and milk drinks at the touch of a button. Incorporating the latest grinding technology, using ceramics and electronics to control the consistency of ground coffee, additional features include click wheel and touch screen controls as well as automatic cup size adjustments. The Platinum range comprises five models as well as the dual drinks maker, the Cappuccino X2.

As a brand, Gaggia continues to move forward. Initiatives such as the Caffe Academie – offering young people hands-on work experience and follow on support within the coffee trade and related industries – demonstrate its commitment to development and evolution. The scheme has attracted attention from leading restaurants, such as Carluccio's and Pizza Express, who acknowledge the long term benefits of providing stimulating training opportunities within the marketplace for young people. As the coffee culture continues to grow, Gaggia is introducing retail concepts in key locations: one-stop shops for coffee, machines, accessories and training.

Gaggia epitomises outstanding design and continuing innovation and while it keeps on producing quality machines and accessories, the UK's growing love affair with coffee shows no sign of abating.

ghd

Adored by women throughout the world, in seven short years, ghd has transformed the lives of millions of devotees through challenging conventions and the power of unshakeable belief.

ghdhair.com

ghd was established in 2001 when its founder, Martin Penny, discovered ceramic hair styling technology. ghd's iconic styling irons were so effective that, despite virtually no marketing, they became an immediate success and initiated a cult following.

The phenomenal growth has intensified; by 2007, revenue had grown from zero to £100 million and ghd is now established in 15 countries – a truly international brand.

ghd's success is built on continued innovation. Never resting, always challenging conventions. Established hair companies have flooded the market with competing irons, yet ghd continues to lead. 2007 saw the launch of the ghd IV styler, ghd's best ever styling iron, but creativity has not been limited to styling irons alone.

In 2006, ghd launched thermodynamics, a complete range of heat styling beauty products, enabling women to make the most of their ghd styler and create new looks.

2007 saw the launch of ghd spa – the world's first range of hair spa products. This collection of premium treatments and products works on the foundations of the hair, creating beauty from within. Only available in the finest spas, ghd spa shows the power of the ghd brand to grow and diversify.

A key decision in the brand's history was to rewrite the rules of the market and only make the products available through the very best professional salons. The elite fell in love with ghd first and word-of-mouth saw women desperately seeking salons that stocked the brand, demanding to own a ghd styler.

Hair is essential to how a woman looks and ghd has used this intrinsic link between hair and fashion to its advantage by sponsoring catwalk collection launches, in addition to styling models for fashion weeks around the world. This unique mix of fashion, style and image amplifies the exclusive, desirable brand positioning.

Salon professionals are still at the heart of everything the brand does. Today ghd runs a unique programme of courses, seminars and events. This year ghd has launched 'Blessed', an exclusive loyalty programme for the very best salons and their clients.

Consumer faith in ghd's products has made 'belief' ghd's brand essence, with the original cult expanding into a much wider following that has been defined as 'a new religion for hair'.

The first salon-only brand to advertise on TV and in fashion titles like Vogue and Elle, ghd's campaigns create consumer demand that can only be satisfied in salons. ghd's campaigns focus on the notion that ghd has a magical, almost supernatural ability to transform the looks and confidence of women. Communications launched in winter 2007 dramatise the self belief that comes with feeling beautiful with unshakeable certainty – 'Thy will be done'.

ghd continues to rewrite the rules with limited editions. The pink styler is a firm favourite and 2008 sees the launch of 'Dark or Pure' special editions, using striking images exclusively shot by Rankin.

GIO-GOI

With its exciting fusion of music and fashion, rock star pals and late night tales, Gio-Goi's street credentials are as authentic as it gets: a brand offering style and credibility for those in the know.

gio-goi.com

Gio-Goi®

Emanating from the transient dance scene of the late 1980s, Gio-Goi has proved itself to be more than a passing fad; two decades on, it is still at the forefront of cutting-edge fashion.

The late 1980s and early 1990s were heady days for the music and club scene. Manchester's Hacienda led the way, with sounds from the likes of the Happy Mondays immortalised by Factory Records; it was into this influential youth culture that the Gio-Goi label tapped. Having previously dabbled in band merchandising, founders Christopher and Anthony Donnelly were given an altogether more challenging brief by Happy Mondays lead singer, Shaun Ryder; to come up with designs that he and his band members would want to wear. It wasn't long before Gio-Goi became the label that key figureheads, in both music and the media, actively sought out. While Brit-pop favourites such as Blur and Oasis became supporters of the brand, Gio-Goi became the uniform of choice for dedicated followers of rave culture, or as it commonly became known, the second 'Summer of Love'.

Today, Gio-Goi (named as the 2007 Drapers Young Fashion Brand of the Year) is worn by a new generation of rock celebrities. Keen advocates such as Tom Meighan of Kasabian, soul sensation Amy Winehouse and indie chart toppers, the Arctic Monkeys, reinforce the strong musical heritage that the brand was built upon. Gio-Goi seasonal collections, across both men's and womenswear, also reflect this long term affinity with youth culture and street attitude, showcasing premium Japanese denims, retro track tops, technical outerwear and throw-over knits – style essentials designed to enable aspiring or discerning rock stars to shift sartorially from day to night.

The brand's appeal owes much to its maverick sense of home-grown style, an eclecticism that continues to attract musicians, actors and sports stars of the moment, many keen to affiliate themselves with a label known for keeping its eye on the ball. In fact, the primary brand goal for Gio-Goi is to become the number one British denim brand – something it is well on its way to achieving.

The unorthodox nature of the brand, and ultimately a big part of its success, comes from its preference for strategic guerrilla-led promotional activity over more conformist forms of marketing. Recent notable and somewhat unconventional activities have included working with revered photographer Mario Testino and musician Pete Doherty, for Vogue Homme; sponsorship of the International Music Summit; partnerships with Cream, Manumission and Ibiza Rocks; headlining the debut Street Rocks and Snow Rocks event in 2009; and staging the exclusive VIP Babyshambles gig at Selfridges. This kind of underground

marketing strategy not only demonstrates the brand's growing kudos, but has also helped to raise the label's profile globally, resulting in increased export distribution across Europe and North America.

Over a period of 20 years, Gio-Goi has forged strong ties with the underground music scene, enabling it to stand out from competitors and helping it to maintain its unique street credibility and brand integrity. The team behind the brand has built up a creative working environment, which fosters the same committed passion and vigour for life and style that its collections convey. 2008 marked two decades for Gio-Goi in the fashion business; a landmark commemorated with new product lines in the premium denim, footwear and accessories categories for Autumn/Winter 2008 as well as an eyewear collection for Spring/Summer 2009.

The name Gio-Goi is Vietnamese in origin, meaning 'to evoke, to excite and to revive', tenets that echo the essence of the brand and embrace the company's continued growth and diversified portfolio.

GREENWICH VILLAGE

Greenwich Village is a global outfit that works with some of the world's most influential design brands, aiming to increase accessibility to contemporary design.

gvuk.co.uk

British-based Greenwich Village was founded in 2003 by brothers Pascal and Stephan Dowers whose vision was to set up the UK's premier design products and interiors company, using its gallery to reach a wider international audience.

Experience gained during their time in London's 1990s club land (as well as time judiciously spent in the bar, gallery and restaurant culture of the early noughties) gave the enterprising siblings invaluable insight into the fast-changing world of cult fads and celebrity culture; they were able to put this to good use when moving into the contemporary design industry.

Anticipating the growing interest in contemporary design was the first major step. Recognising consumers' increasingly demanding and discerning approach to choosing architecture, design and art, the brothers set out to make anticipating trends their particular niche. Over the years Pascal and Stephan have also extended their long-held appreciation of art and design into a further range of businesses and projects. For instance, during 1999 and 2000 they restored the oldest existing music hall in the UK, in Greenwich, into a double

Time Out and Perrier award-winning bar-meets-restaurant-meets-gallery, stylishly complementing the existing Georgian decor with one of the largest collections of modern classic furniture in London at that time.

When the brothers first ventured into the design industry they saw it as fragmented, with the consumer often badly served. Careful analysis of the UK market and the companies and products on offer, guided the pair into choosing what they believed were the right designers for their newly launched company; knowing which designers to pick and develop is a skill that Greenwich Village has exploited with the likes of the Campana Brothers and Studio Job. In 2003, finding no takers to produce the Campana's 'toy banquette' the brand launched its Greenwich Village Gallery specialising in eclectic design (www.designartgallery.co.uk). Since then Greenwich Village

has been at the forefront of this rapidly growing market with its annual SuperDesign event, timed to coincide with the Frieze Art Fair, attended by the world's leading contemporary art collectors. During the last three years the brand has been influential across the industry with its cutting-edge products filling the pages of design and interior magazines.

In order to facilitate and ensure the brand's success the right premises were crucial; a big enough space in which to showcase products effectively that would also attract central London clientele. The brand opened its Greenwich-based 5,000 sq ft office, warehouse and showroom in March 2004, the main focus of which was to offer a service to interior designers, architects and the 'contract' market. Following on its heels was a search for the perfect consumer outlet; the brothers chose Selfridges. Although it had a reputation for fashion its furniture offering was a little on the staid side,

providing the perfect backdrop for the emerging Greenwich Village brand which opened its London concession in Selfridges in April 2005.

Greenwich Village has already built up a network of collaborators worldwide, presenting shows in Tokyo and other international locations within a short time span. The brand's future plans centre on the continued development of the Greenwich Village designers stable, with more work planned in the UK and new presentations worldwide, from New York to the Middle East, and a prominent permanent gallery space due to open imminently in London.

The Dowers brothers believe in presenting a 'show', effectively putting entertainment into the traditionally conservative world of art – a brave move, but to date an effective one. The forthcoming year will see them concentrating their efforts on the gallery arena and top level interiors.

GROLSCH

With centuries of brewing behind it, Grolsch's Dutch heritage plays a fundamental part in defining both its brand values and customers: laid-back, intelligent and free-thinking.

You have to go back to 1615 to uncover the history of Grolsch when Peter Cuyper, its founding father, first came upon the delicate balance of ingredients that give the brand its distinctive flavour.

The brand's name is drawn from the location of its first brewery, in a Dutch town called Groenlo, meaning 'green wood or forest': a literal translation of Grolsch being 'beer from the green wood'.

Grolsch encapsulates the Dutch laid-back approach to life, albeit with a quirky edge. While unwilling to give away trade secrets, its characteristics – namely a full-body, crisp flavour, golden colour, naturally high carbonation and creamy head – rely on soft water, extracted from a 600-foot well, and a protracted brewing process. This long brewing process (and unusual ingredients such as the Hallertau Perle hops, added later than other hops to give Grolsch a unique aroma) is indicative of the brand's unconventional approach.

The Grolsch Swingtop, also in keeping with the brand's non-conformist outlook, has established itself over recent decades as an iconic design, further elevating the beer's 'cool' status. The bottle design (like the brand's brewing process) has longevity, being modified only four times since its introduction in 1897. The latest design, displayed in the Museum of Brands, Packaging and Advertising in London, reflects the brand's authenticity and key qualities of innovation, originality, independence and individuality.

In 1988, Grolsch decided to replace its two existing breweries with one flagship operation, better equipped to deal with growing demand and also capable of combining its brewing heritage with state-of-the-art technology – simultaneously improving both the brand's production efficiency and eco-credentials. The new brewery is one of the most up-to-date in the world and opened on 7th April 2004 in south-west Enschede, Holland. Environmental measures, including lower water and energy consumption, were part of the brief and demonstrate the brand's forward-thinking approach to production.

Across 2007 and 2008, Grolsch added two new brand extensions to its UK portfolio: Grolsch Weizen and Grolsch Blond. While Blond uses the same ingredients as Grolsch Lager it is brewed to a lighter tasting four per cent, giving it a crisp, thirst-quenching appeal. Grolsch Weizen, meanwhile, was initially brewed to celebrate the opening of the brewery in Enschede but proved so popular that the brand decided to keep making it; a well-advised decision, given that it scooped the title of 'World's Best Wheat Beer' at the 2007 World Beer Awards.

Since January 2008, Grolsch has sponsored original comedy on Channel 4 that includes hit British shows such as The Friday Night Project, 8 Out of 10 Cats and Peep Show. The sponsorship idents feature two Dutchmen reclining on the grass-covered roof of a barge in Amsterdam. As they wile away the hours on the canal with Grolsch, their surreal, light-hearted banter conveys the brand's own laid-back, idiosyncratic personality. The campaign, supported by heavy weight below-the-line activity, has already had an impact on raising brand awareness.

Further brand promotion centres on recreating the bustling, continental outdoor drinking vibe that the Dutch (ergo Grolsch) are famed for. During the 2008 Edinburgh Festival, for instance, the pasture outside E4's Udderbelly venue was revamped with a Dutch-style outdoor service offering a range of Grolsch beers. The scene emulated the brand's multi award-winning 'Welcome to the Green Light District' experiential campaign, in which some of the UK's trendiest bars were given an overhaul to offer a taster of the quintessential Dutch drinking experience.

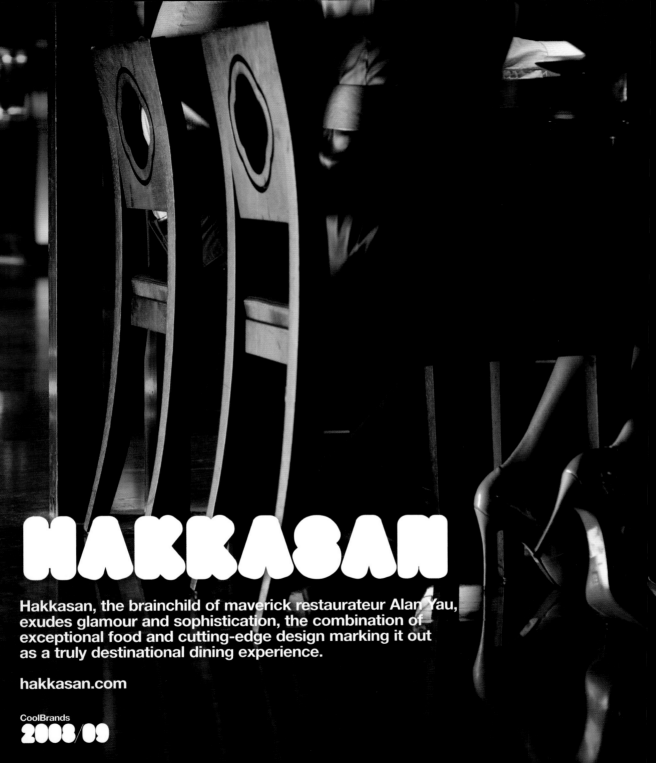

HAKKASAN

Hakkasan, the brainchild of maverick restaurateur Alan Yau, exudes glamour and sophistication, the combination of exceptional food and cutting-edge design marking it out as a truly destinational dining experience.

hakkasan.com

haᐟkasan

The challenge: to create a Chinese restaurant in London's West End to equal the substance and style of leading establishments in Hong Kong and Singapore. The result: Hakkasan.

The restaurant's decadent interior – intimately divided with dark-wood lattice screens, bathed in an electric blue glow – is the work of accredited designer Christian Liaigre, favoured by fashionistas and responsible for the homes of Karl Lagerfeld and Calvin Klein, as well as New York's ultra-hip Mercer Hotel. Yau's brief to Liaigre was to 'bring back the dragon', namely to create a modern but distinctly ethnic interior. The designer responded by fusing an avant-garde modern aesthetic with traditional Chinese emblems and motifs.

Hakkasan's interior consists of three distinct areas: a main dining room that seats 145; a lounge styled area; and a 16 metre long bar, made from dark-stained English oak. The same dark wood has been used on the tables in sharp contrast to the lighter tones of blue glass and green slate surrounding the walls. A wall of sawn slate provides a dramatic background for nocturnal bar activity, separated from the more tranquil setting of the dining area. Oriental wooden screens (decorated with contemporary geometric designs) form a 'cage' around the main dining room, providing tantalising glimpses of fellow diners as well as the bar and lounge beyond.

The restaurant's modest surroundings – on a side street, just steps away from the bustle of Oxford Street – belie the allure that typifies Liaigre's distinctive style, often described simply as 'sexy'. Descending the incense-infused stairs into the artfully illuminated

subterranean world (put together by acclaimed lighting designer Arnold Chan of Isometrix) has been likened by some to passing from day to night, or from this world into another. With ambience playing such a pivotal role, a CD is currently in production, setting out to capture the Hakkasan mood within music.

The kitchen, partially visible from the restaurant, adds a further theatrical eloquence to the experience, with the chefs intrinsically part of the occasion. Experienced head chef, Tong Chee Hwee, works with a strong team – including sous chef and master dim sum chef – whom he brought with him from the renowned Summer Pavilion Chinese restaurant at the Ritz Carlton in Singapore. Together they have created a modern authentic Cantonese menu, with dishes that have been modified only slightly in order that they retain their Chinese authenticity.

Hakkasan's reputation was sealed when it acquired a Michelin star in 2003, which it has retained ever since. In the same year, it walked away with the award for 'Outstanding Contribution to London Restaurants' at the Moët & Chandon London Restaurant Awards. Hakkasan continues to receive awards and industry recognition. In April 2008, The S. Pellegrino World's 50 Best Restaurants annual list rated Hakkasan 19th, one of only five London restaurants to make the rankings.

In 2006, founder Alan Yau was awarded an OBE from the Queen for his 'contribution to the British restaurant industry'. But such success has not made Yau rest on his laurels; his ambition to roll-out Hakkasan as a global brand moved a step forward in February 2008, with the launch of a rooftop eaterie in Istanbul. This opening is to be followed by two further restaurants in Miami and Abu Dhabi by the year-end, with menus specifically tailored to meet local tastes, while plans are in the pipeline for further restaurants in Las Vegas, China and the Middle East.

HEAL'S

Renowned as much for its innovation as it is for its British heritage, Heal's prides itself on a commitment to enduring quality and expert home-grown craftsmanship.

heals.co.uk

HEAL'S

Heal's builds on almost 200 years of design tradition by embracing change and establishing the right balance between trust, value, choice and individuality.

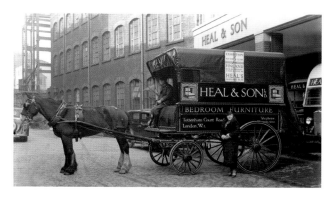

Heal's dates back to 1810, when John Harris Heal established the family-run business, initially as a bed-making firm. In 1840 his son took over the reins, even then displaying the brand's pioneering spirit by placing adverts in seven of Charles Dickens' novels. The business, already a household name, expanded its product offering to include bedroom furniture as well.

In 1893 Ambrose Heal joined the company, designing and making simple furniture. His avid interest in typography led to the brand's first furniture catalogue, in 1898, exemplifying its definitive style. Ambrose's contribution, both to the business and to British furniture, has been universally acknowledged through a host of industry awards.

Heal's has been a presence on London's Tottenham Court Road since 1840. The central part of the existing building, commissioned by Ambrose and designed by Cecil Brewer, was hailed as a landmark in shop architecture following its completion in 1917.

In 1960, as part of its 150th anniversary celebrations, Heal's launched its Designers of the Future Exhibition, commissioning young designers from seven European countries to design a room in the building's Mansard Gallery. This marked the start of the brand's long tradition of investing in and nurturing new design talent, still evident to this day through the annual Heal's Discovers collection. Since launch it has pioneered the work of 36 new designers, winning accolades from the V&A, Homes and Gardens magazine and Elle Decoration. It has also given rise to some enduring collaborations, such

as that with John Reeves: a finalist in Heal's Discovers 2005, Reeves has gone on to create the Louis range for the store, with further additions to be launched in 2008. Recent collaborations with more established designers include an exclusive new range of furniture from Orla Kiely.

In 1984, Heal's was bought by Terence Conran, under the Storehouse Group umbrella. The Storehouse chain store mentality proved to be at odds with the brand, resulting in a management buyout during the late 1980s recession which paved the way for a radical reinvention; most of the product

lines, for instance, changed to new exclusive ranges designed expressly for Heal's, displaying the quality and craftsmanship the brand was founded on. During the second half of the 1990s, Heal's once again began to expand, opening two new stores – on Chelsea's King's Road and in Kingston upon Thames – and launching a website in November 2000, in time for Christmas trading and the new millennium.

Following a further buyout by Wittington Investments Limited in 2001, Heal's has undergone a further transformation in recent years with new branding, product lines and services, all marketed through a fresh brand campaign that reflects its commitment to quality and an ability to adapt to changing tastes: a quintessentially British trait.

Innovation has always been part of the Heal's ethos and in line with an extensive refurbishment of its Tottenham Court Road flagship store in 2006, it launched a host of new services, including: interior design; bespoke furniture, rugs, curtains and blinds; an online wedding and gift list service; and an in-store catering offering – the Meals restaurant and the Oliver Peyton bakery.

In the last five years Heal's has continued its expansion policy, opening new stores in Manchester, Leeds and Brighton – its first seaside location. Future plans include further store openings across the UK along with an extensive online range of furniture and related products.

KÉRASTASE

To constantly innovate in order to bring the salon experience to new levels of luxury and expertise: this is the mission of leading professional hair care brand Kérastase.

kerastase.co.uk

CoolBrands
2008/09

KÉRASTASE
PARIS

Since its creation in 1964, Kérastase has become a cult brand for millions of women worldwide, as well as thousands of the most influential professional hairdressers, celebrities and beauty journalists.

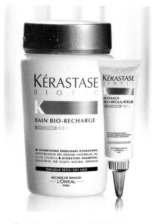

Over the years, Kérastase's impeccable credentials have resulted in extensive consumer and professional recognition; the most recent additions to its armoury of beauty awards include an unprecedented five products being celebrated at the 2008 InStyle Awards. In addition, Noctogenist won the coveted 'Best New Professional Haircare Product – Prestige' at the 2008 Cosmetic Executive Women UK Beauty Awards, voted for by the most influential women in the beauty industry.

Kérastase has a strong heritage: originally making its mark in the 1960s by launching revolutionary in-salon products to cleanse and purify the scalp, key partnerships with some of the world's top hairdressers and salons were forged. Nurturing these relationships over the years has enabled Kérastase to aim for the ultimate in luxurious hair care experiences and to develop innovative products and services.

Remaining aware of its customers' changing needs, the brand has continued to break the boundaries in its collections. In the 1970s its first professional homecare products were introduced, as women increasingly washed their hair at home and hairstyle trends became more extravagant. The 1980s saw the launch of the first complete collection for dry hair and the first sun hair care containing UV filters. In the 1990s, Kérastase personalised its range further with hair masques for fine or thick hair and introduced breakthrough technology and ingredients from L'Oréal's Advanced Research, such as ceramides and Vita-Ciment®.

Since its introduction to the market, Kérastase has placed the hairdresser at the heart of its philosophy. As early as 1964, the hair stylist became an advocate for the brand in the salon, looking to the products' technology in order to prescribe the correct product for their customers' individual hair needs. Today, Kérastase is proud to have an established network of Ambassadors throughout the UK – a community of top hairdressers who understand the benefits of the tailor-made solutions that Kérastase products can offer their clients.

From its early days, Kérastase realised the importance of encouraging the hairdressing profession to be at the forefront of change, to focus on developing and implementing a new vision for a hairdressing salon: an environment geared towards total relaxation while providing the most advanced hair and scalp treatments. At Kérastase, this emphasis on education and environment is seen as playing a crucial role in elevating the customer experience and further establishing the brand's luxury positioning, as well as driving growth in the market.

In 2007, Kérastase launched Ciment Thermique, a heat-activated fortifying milk for weakened hair. The product became an instant beauty must-have for women looking to style their hair more quickly, while simultaneously nourishing and repairing it. One year later, Kérastase took the market by storm once again with Noctogenist, the first tailored night treatment to revitalise dull and tired-looking hair.

In July 2008, the brand again broke the boundaries of salon hair care: inspired by the world of pre- and pro-biotics – a key trend within the food industry – Kérastase launched Biotic, a preventative and solutional approach to hair beauty. Offering both Scalp Insurance – to maintain healthy defence systems to prevent scalp irritations from occurring – and a Controlling Action, to rebalance the scalp completely and reactivate its natural defences, Biotic marks a new direction for the brand.

With high performance prescriptive products and innovative technologies, as well as a presence in some of the world's most beautiful salons, Kérastase continues to be the leading professional luxury hair care brand in the world, a symbol of timeless elegance and hair beauty.

KIEHL'S

Kiehl's is an original New York pharmacy that offers a range of skin care, hair care and body care products with an emphasis on uncompromising quality, often using naturally derived ingredients.

kiehls.com

KIEHL'S 1851
NDULA HERBAL-EXTRACT T
Alcohol-Free
with Whole Flowers and Pure Ext

toner is formulated with select herbal extracts to gently cleanse and s
types without the use of alcohol or harsh synthetic drying agents. O
t Toner may be used to improve the appearance of acne blemis
ations and is also often recommended for use after shaving.

*S: Before applying, we recommend patch-testing a small an
t on the inside bend of the elbow or on the inside skin of the w
compatibility with your skin. For detailed patch-testing instruc
chure or hand-out. Moisten a sterile cotton pad with toner, and
eeded, avoiding the eye area.*

Keep Out of Eyes and Immediate Eye Areas. If Contact with I
Thoroughly with Water and Consult a Physician. Keep Out
Not Intended for Use on Children. Do Not Swallow: Not Intended
se of Accidental Ingestion, Seek Medical Assistance or Cont
ater Immediately. If Rash or Irritation Occurs, Remove Produ
Applied, Discontinue Use and Consult a Physician.
INGREDIENTS: Aqueous Extract of Calendula Officinalis, P
Extract, Burdock Extract, Ivy Extract, Gentian Extract, Imu
, Allantoin, Comfrey Extract

Kiehl's Since 1851, Inc.® • New York, NY 10003
further information, please call 1-800-KIEHLS-1 (1-800-543-

net 8 fl. oz

6 13431

KIEHL'S 1851
AMINO ACID
SHAMPOO
with Pure Coconut Oil

oduct contains Amino Acid cleansen
gently and effectively cleanse the hair

ad and Pure Coconut Oil derived cle
eamy lather that gently yet thorough
d Starch help add body and fullnes
nts impart softness and shine. Su
desired.

ly massage a small amount throughout th
the Kiehl's Conditioner or Styling Aid of
TS: Water/Aqua, Sodium Methyl Co
hloride, Coco-Betaine, Fragrance/Parfum
cylic Acid, Guar Hydroxypropyltrimoni
ol, Methylparaben, Coconut Oil/Coc
cids, Ethylparaben, Hydrolyzed Wh
Quillaja Saponaria Bark Extract, Hy

ct should only be used on speci
ut of reach of children. If disc
e use and consult a physician

h's Since 1851 LLC • Ne
MADE IN U.S
l's Canada, Mc
www.kiehls.cc
Not Tested On

fl. oz. - 125

KIEHL'S 1851
ULTRA FACIAL
MOISTURIZER
for all skin types

oisturizer is readily absorbed under the facial skin
e area soft and nurtured. Th
of this formulat
layers for
urizing of the sk
ge a small amou
ediate eye area.
This product sh
cted. As a general
discomfort or sensi
e and consult a ph
Broschüre.)

.4 fl. oz. - 250

Kiehl's LIP
BALM #1
SPF 4 Sunscreen
Petrolatum Lip
Protectant

Temporarily protects and
helps relieve chapped
or cracked lips. Helps
protect lips from the
drying effects of wind
and cold weather. Apply

06ACWC   1400068

SINCE KIE
BLUE A
HERB.
Formula
This product is n

This unique form
use after shaving

DIRECTIONS: M
toner, and apply to s
contact with eyes.
The Kiehl's Patch-Te

Kiehl's
SINCE 1851

Established as an old-world apothecary in New York's East Village neighbourhood more than 150 years ago, Kiehl's is infused with a blend of cosmetic, pharmaceutical, herbal, and medicinal knowledge developed through generations.

During the first half of the 20th century the brand was a pharmacy, offering homeopathic and herbal remedies, essential oils, over the counter drugs, and fledgling own-brand products. During the early 1960s, through utilising the knowledge and expertise gained from its experience in pharmaceutical manufacturing and chemistry, it began to develop its own product range and is today dedicated to offering an extensive line of high quality skin and hair care formulations. The Dermatologist Solutions range, for example, is a direct response to consumer demand for increasingly sophisticated skin care products. Developed in collaboration with leading dermatologists, the range includes effective targeted treatments such as Powerful-Strength Line Reducing Concentrate and Over-Night Biological Peel. Kiehl's also established an Endowed Fund for Skin Cancer Research in 1999 with post-doctoral students at the Harvard Center for Cancer Biology.

The brand has a no-frills approach to packaging and this, coupled with its emphasis on word-of-mouth recommendation as reflected in its generous 'try before you buy' sampling policy, enables the company to channel its resources into the very best product formulations and philanthropic causes, something which has helped to build a loyal international fan-base.

All Kiehl's customer representatives undergo an intensive education program to learn the value and effectiveness of formula ingredients; a demonstration of the brand's commitment to quality.

Building on its early traditions in dispensing advice on prescriptions, staff continue to 'prescribe' a personally devised care regimen, with brand information made readily available.

Educating customers on maintaining active, healthy lifestyles is key to the Kiehl's philosophy, with the brand embracing activities such as aviation, alpine ski racing, equestrianism and motorcycling during its history. Over the years, these passions and interests have become part of the visual and emotional fabric of the company; perhaps best represented by the company's collection of vintage motorcycles displayed in Kiehl's stores worldwide.

The company's values are ensconced in 'The Mission of Kiehl's Since 1851', written more than 30 years ago, which clearly outlines its commitment to giving back to the communities in which it serves. Its partnership with the Targanine Women's Co-operative in Morocco's Atlas Mountains region – the source of the organic and fairly-traded Argan oil used in its new Superbly Restorative Preparations range – helps to provide the women who work for it with a source of dependable income, as well as a means of improving access to healthcare and education. The environmentally friendly bottles in this range are composed of 100 per cent post-consumer recycled (PCR) plastic.

Charitable support is also a cornerstone of its philosophy and since 2002 Kiehl's has worked closely with Terrence Higgins Trust (THT) in the UK, from sponsoring events to selling limited edition products. 2008 sees Kiehl's lend its support to World AIDS Day, with an exclusive version of Lip Balm #1 (featuring the iconic red ribbon on its packaging) and in-store fundraisers generating additional funds for THT.

Since its inception, Kiehl's has formulated products to target specific customer needs, for both women and men, with iconic products including Creme de Corps, Lip Balm #1 and Ultra Facial Moisturiser. While most formulations are considered to be unisex, popular products aimed specifically at men include White Eagle Shave Cream and Blue Astringent Herbal Toner, as well as new favourites Facial Fuel Moisturiser and Ultimate Strength Hand Salve. In recent years the brand's male customer base has grown to become one of the industry's largest, showing the combination of advanced technology and naturally-derived ingredients to be a recipe for success.

LAST.FM

United by the desire to spread the musical message and live life with a soundtrack, the people behind Last.fm have created a home for passionate online music fans.

last.fm

last.fm

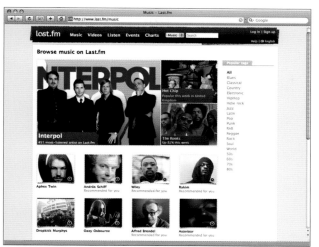

Lack of financing didn't prevent Felix Miller, Martin Stiksel and Richard Jones from founding a free music website in 2002. Since then Last.fm has built up a global community of more than 21 million music fans.

Last.fm's founding principle is a love of music; whether it is through music listening, sharing or discovery, this remains the driving force. Music fans are able to enjoy more than five million tracks from all musical genres that can be accessed for free, either on demand, or through personalised radio stations. The overall commitment is to entertainment, with a comprehensive music information service giving access to artist pictures, videos, charts, discographies and concert listings thrown in for good measure.

Last.fm uses a unique technology that tracks what users listen to through iTunes, iPods and other media players, so music profiles are always up-to-date. It can then compare a user's musical taste to that of millions of others within its community, thereby accurately recommending new music in line with individual preferences. Unlike other recommendation services, Last.fm's music discovery system is based on what people are really listening to, enabling it to tailor recommendations.

Despite its unorthodox start-up – with the first employees sleeping on the office roof in a tent and relying on Felix's culinary skills – a passion for music guided the brand through its first few years and attracted more like-minded employees; its 100-strong team now includes DJs, musicians, writers, artists, and a talking robot.

Located in central London (the birthplace of musical revolutions such as The British Invasion, Ska, Punk, Acid House and BritPop), Last.fm's base near the Old Street Roundabout – recently dubbed 'London's answer to Silicon Valley' – mirrors the cornerstones of the brand: music, technology and fun.

As a social brand built on user-generated content, many of Last.fm's early initiatives relied on users for viral spread; one of the most successful being users' personal charts, which could be embedded as a widget into blogs or web pages and displayed the user's current favourite listening choices. Brand extensions now include a Facebook application, which displays current listening and updates in real time, www.playground.last.fm (a virtual lab where new ideas are tested out), www.build.last.fm – a gallery of applications built by the community – and iPhone applications, allowing iPhone and iPod Touch users to access Last.fm on the move.

In 2007, Last.fm launched Last.fm/Presents, an original content channel dedicated to interviews and live performances from some of the best new bands, and has already put on concerts in London and New York and interviewed artists such as Moby, Portishead, Santogold and Steve Aoki.

Last.fm reached 15 million users before being acquired by CBS for $280 million in 2007. Working with CBS, Last.fm is providing an online destination for the music fans amongst TV viewers, enabling them to listen again to music from popular shows like the Grammys, thus extending the TV experience.

The Last.fm logo has a humanist feel symbolising the strong social aspect of the brand. The connected letters represent the data transfer from music listeners to Last.fm and stand for the growth of the site through user-generated content, which has bagged the brand a number of industry accolades including the Webby Award for Music in 2007, the top spot in the Audio category of the 2008 Webware 100, and winning the Music category of the SEOmoz Web 2.0 Awards in the same year.

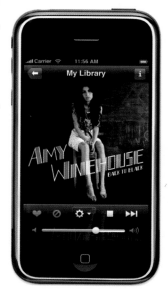

LG

LG Electronics is a worldwide
technology and design leader in
mobile communications, employing
over 82,000 people in more than
110 operations, including 81
subsidiaries worldwide.

lge.com

As consumer awareness of the LG brand and its products has increased, so too has the brand's reputation for design and innovation through premium technology that is helping to shape the electronics industry.

With consumer loyalty increasingly dictated by how a brand makes a consumer feel and the benefits it offers, rather than product allegiance, LG recently invested more than $150 million into making the brand more accessible, distinctive and relevant to its target audience.

LG's marketing campaigns, designed to help consumers identify with the brand by specific targeting, use a range of different media including search engine marketing, online banner advertisements, cinema advertising and dedicated websites. Current product campaigns include the 9kg Steam Washer, the Secret mobile handset and the Scarlet LCD TV, the launch of which masqueraded as the première of a new TV series by David Nutter.

LG's high-profile sponsorships are designed to engage customers further: on a global scale, the likes of The International Cricket Council, Action Sports, the 2008 FIS Snowboarding World Championships and P1 Powerboat World Championships; and on the domestic front, London Fashion Week, Fulham FC and Arsenal FC. In addition, the brand is lead sponsor of a snowboarding and festival style event (the first of its kind) held at Battersea Power Station – 'Freesports on 4 FREEZE, sponsored by LG' – which is also set to host the FIS Snowboard World Cup for the first time in London. Raising brand awareness at premier events remains a key brand focus, from the technology-led, such as the Consumer Electronics Show and Mobile World Congress to lifestyle and fashion events such as the Cannes Film Festival and Ideal Home Show. One of its latest collaborations involves the redesign and renaming of Birmingham's NEC Arena to the LG Arena.

Engagement through media experiences also plays a major part in LG's marketing strategy, its first full high definition TV range for instance, was launched at a star-studded press event featuring Lily Allen and Primal Scream's Bobby Gillespie. 2008 has so far seen Secret launched at London celebrity hotspot Sketch, featuring DJ Jeremy Healey, and the long awaited opening of the Harrods LG Lounge (previously the i-Gallery), designed to showcase LG products and increase consumer interactivity with the brand.

The LG logo – consisting of two elements, the LG letterforms in grey and the face symbol in red – is designed to symbolise the world, future, youth, humanity, and technology. The company's philosophy, based on humanity, is highlighted by its commitment to promoting sustainability and building relationships with the local communities it works with. As a company LG has led the way in Corporate Social Responsibility, implementing a wide range of programmes that includes a 'Fight Against Cancer' campaign in France, the 'Thai Forever' anti-drug campaign, and China's 'LG Screen Connects You & Me' project.

LG differs from many other electronic brands by using its insight and expertise in smart technology and stylish design to create new solutions to life's challenges; hence its slogan, 'Life's Good'. Washers in the LG Steam range, for example, use steam instead of water to save energy, lower water consumption and remove allergens and creases from clothes – as well as saving time.

LG has grown exponentially in recent years, recording many industry firsts along the way and scooping numerous awards. In 2007 its landmark Super Multi Blue player won 'Most Innovative Gadget of the Year' at the first T3 Gadget Awards, while the same year saw LG collect three trophies from the prestigious European Imaging and Sound Association (EISA) Awards for its design-led home entertainment products. Such sucess shows no signs of abating, with LG's Home Theatre system, tuned by high-end audio systems specialist Mark Levinson, winning the EISA award for 'European Home Theatre System 2008/09'.

MADAME V

Aimed at today's new breed of sophisticated woman, Madame V is a luxury sensual lifestyle brand that blends high quality designer lingerie, loungewear and accessories with the art of seduction.

madamev.co.uk

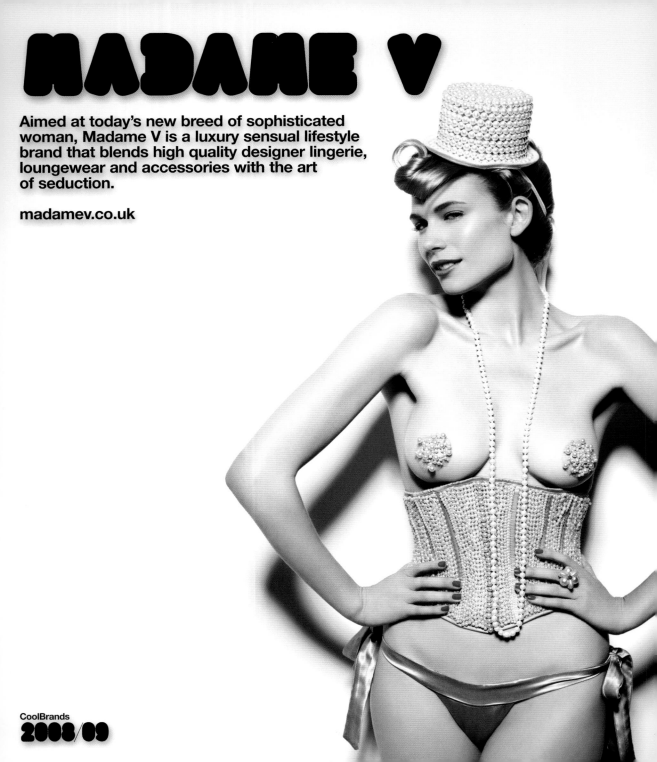

MADAME V

Madame V, which made its UK debut in 2002, strives to dispel the myths and taboos around sex by encouraging people to introduce seduction and sensuality into their everyday lives.

While women today are ever more sophisticated and self-assured in their sexuality (being more empowered now than perhaps at any other time in recent history), many find that they have less time for both themselves and their relationships. Madame V challenges common perceptions of sensuality and through a range of titillating products, targeted at both female and male customers, offers ways in which it can be accommodated – into any lifestyle.

This lifestyle approach to seduction is reflected through a variety of luxury lingerie, including loungewear, under and outerwear, accessories and bedroom products, designed across four distinct collections. Each of the collections – Classica, Romantica, Viva and Femme Fatale – is unique, the concepts designed to appeal to different tastes and personal moods. While some designs have a distinctly playful and burlesque appeal (and others combine eroticism with fashion), all maintain a level of sophistication in keeping with the brand's philosophy.

The Madame V head office and showroom, located in central London, reflects the brand's key aim: to be at the forefront of fashion and seduction while continually expanding and looking at new and radical ways of innovating, in both traditional lingerie design and in the range of materials and quality of fabrics used. Madame V's product offering relies on this exacting quality, achieved through retaining strict and personal

control over its product (and brand image) through its dynamic and creative in-house design, production, sales and marketing teams. Most of the designs that exude old-style glamour use distinctive fabrics and are, in the main, hand-finished in the brand's own factory in order to ensure that its characteristic quality is maintained.

Since its launch, Madame V has been involved in a range of high-profile projects and events, including Selfridges' '40 Brasil' store concept and joining forces with Godiva Chocolatiers to launch its celebratory 75th anniversary campaign. As a rapidly expanding global brand Madame V is now stocked by some of the leading international stores such as Harrods UK, Coco de Mer, Harvey Nichols Dubai, 11 Corso Como and Clube Chocolate Brazil.

In 2004 Madame V launched its flagship store in the heart of Milan and is currently finalising plans for further key stores in prime locations across Europe. While a cohesive marketing strategy undeniably plays a significant role in the brand's expansion, Madame V's reputation has been established on the back of its seductive product range, which since its launch has featured heavily in top UK and international publications such as British Vogue, British Elle, Tatler, Harper's Bazaar, I-D, The Times, the Guardian, the FT's How to Spend It, Sunday Times Style, The Independent, The Evening Standard, the Daily Mail, Vogue (Russia), Vogue (Japan), Elle

(Italy), Glamour (Italy), GQ, Arena and VOGUE.COM.

At the heart of Madame V is love and this is ultimately what continues to guide and direct the brand's provocative and inspirational collections. Aspiring to be the ultimate London-based luxury seduction lifestyle brand, Madame V aims to ensure that its products provoke an emotional response and put the customer on the path to lavish living.

PERRIER

Sourced from a spring in south-west France, more than 800 million distinctively shaped bottles of Perrier mineral water are produced each year. Distributed to more than 140 countries, it is a symbol of natural refreshment.

perrier.com

It was Napoleon III who first granted permission for spring water from Les Bouillens to be bottled, back in 1863. But it was another 40 years before the Perrier story really began.

In 1898, Dr Louis Perrier took ownership of the Bouillens estate, the source of Perrier's spring water. Setting up a medical practice in the nearby ancient Roman town of Nîmes, he began the tough challenge of selling bottled water to the French – a nation at that time more drawn towards the intoxicating flavours of wine and absinthe.

A chance meeting in 1902, with a young Englishman, John Harmsworth, marked the beginning of the Perrier brand. Dr Perrier sold his Bouillens estate to Harmsworth, who named the spring after the doctor in recognition of his tireless efforts to establish the bottled water business. Today 1,200 people are employed at the factory where Dr Perrier and Harmsworth are remembered, both for the roles they played in developing the company and for the legacy they left: a strong brand image.

Part of this brand identity is the Perrier logo, dating back to the 1930s. Although Perrier's corporate identity has since been updated to a more contemporary feel, it still draws on the brand's heritage. Both the trademark glass bottle and logo – comprising a faded dark green, golden textured wings and a touch of silver – reflect the product's past and emphasise its premium nature. In line with developing the brand's contemporary edge, recent years have seen designers including Custo Barcelona and agnès b. create limited edition Perrier packaging. In winter 2007, the Paul & Joe label dressed the distinctive green bottle in three bespoke designs.

Perrier is a natural mineral water, as defined by French law, meaning it has a stable composition and healthy properties. The water in all bottled Perrier comes from an underground source and contains only mineral salts and carbonation, making it calorie free. To ensure the intensity of the bubbles, the carbonic gas from the spring is tapped separately from deep within the source before being added to the water at the bottling stage.

Between the years of 1987 and 1992, when Perrier launched its flavoured waters – made from natural mineral water and flavourings – on both the US and French markets, sales of the brand rocketed, reaching one billion bottles worldwide in 1988. In 1991, Perrier revamped its marketing campaign to focus primarily on the water, enlisting creatives such as Jean Paul Goude and Ridley Scott to convey Perrier's qualities across various mediums. Memorable slogans such as 'Perrier c'est fou!' and 'L'eau, l'air, la vie, Perrier…' have since become synonymous with the brand.

THE BOUNCE
1/3 Perrier + 2/3 Perrier

Enjoy Perrier straight, with a slice of lemon, very cold but without ice. A sophisticated and refreshing alternative to ordinary sparkling drinks. REFRESHINGLY UNIQUE

UK marketing of Perrier has also been built around its central asset – water, or more accurately, eau – with a series of inter-linked adverts gaining cult status: 'Eau–la-la', 'Eau Noveau', 'Bistreau','Picasseau', 'Rainbeau', and 'H2Eau'. The brand's current 'Cocktail Campaign' continues this strategy while strengthening its positioning as an alternative to carbonated soft drinks and alcohol. Under the banner of 'Refreshingly Unique', Perrier 'cocktails' – containing only Perrier – are served in a somewhat surreal bar setting.

Over the years, Perrier has been the proud recipient of a Royal Warrant from no fewer than three Royal Households: King Edward VII, King George V, and the King of Spain. Its advertising campaigns have also picked up several prestigious awards such as the Grand Prix de l'Affichage. As the official water for the Roland Garros French Open, Perrier's status as the leading French mineral water is undisputed and its long tradition of providing a premium sparkling water continues.

PLAY.COM

The UK's number one online retailer, PLAY.COM offers its customers a comprehensive choice of products, award-winning service, accessibility and an unwavering commitment to uphold its 'free delivery on everything' policy.

play.com

PLAY.COM is a revolutionary retailer offering a vast range of music, games, film, mobiles, books, gadgets, electricals and clothing. It offers free delivery on everything, which is one reason why its customer service is award-winning.

PLAY.COM started life as play247.com more than 10 years ago, during an age when people were still saying things like: "Have you ever heard of Digital Versatile Discs? They might be the next big thing. Or they may go the way of the laser discs." It was during this time that two born and raised Jersey islanders decided they might try to sell them through a mail order catalogue. These new-fangled Digital Versatile Discs (the now familiar DVDs) proved to be a success, so they decided to use the internet – also still in its infancy – as their selling platform. In creating a website they established a digital version of their catalogue, which proved to be a major turning point for the company as sales quadrupled overnight.

The site has continued to be a success due to the vision of its founders. They placed emphasis on the content of the site, with well-researched information about each of the DVDs a priority. In order to gain customer support above and beyond any of their competitors, they decided to stock every DVD release from 'Railways of Southern Wales' to 'Batman: The Dark Knight' while making a website that was fluent, welcoming and user friendly. In addition to this, they also realised how important price had become to consumers so aimed to make all prices unbeatable. This foresight has served the islanders well and PLAY.COM is now a huge presence for online retail in Europe. Its original team of 10 has become a team of more than 700.

Today, PLAY.COM has more than six million products listed on the site and acts as a one-stop shop for a vast range of entertainment needs. From blockbuster DVDs, chart CDs and music downloads to next generation games consoles and games, as well as high definition LCD TVs and MP3 players,

all significantly cheaper than on the high street. Furthermore, PLAY.COM offers books ranging from the year's bestselling paperbacks to collectors' editions, as well as thousands of gadgets and gizmos and a new clothing range. As PLAY.COM's range has increased, its policy of not charging for postage and packing has remained the same – it is always completely free on everything. Items that are in stock are usually dispatched within 24 hours and delivered within 1-3 working days. Its customer service through telephone and email aims to ensure that every customer has a stress-free buying experience.

The brand has been a consistent award winner, most recently picking up 'Best Online Store' at the Which Awards 2008. Its many other accolades include: topping the ABA Research and Foresee Customer Satisfaction Surveys in 2007; winning the British

Video Association's 'Retail Success of the Year' award each year from 2004 to 2007; and being named Hitwise's 'Number One Website' in both the Video & Games and Music categories annually since 2004. PLAY.COM was also short-listed at the 2007 Bookseller Retail Awards in the Direct to Consumer Bookselling Company of the Year category.

PLAY.COM has played a key role in revolutionising the way leisure and entertainment products are purchased. As next generation technology and entertainment are developed, PLAY.COM will undoubtedly be at the forefront in delivering it to the consumer.

REGGAE REGGAE SAUCE

By putting the fun into Caribbean food, Levi Roots – the charismatic face behind Reggae Reggae Sauce – is increasing appreciation and accessibility of this popular cuisine within the UK.

reggae-reggae.co.uk

For Levi Roots, the creator of Reggae Reggae Sauce, winning over the business minds of the Dragons' Den with just a song and a smile was only the start.

It was in 2006 that the Brixton-based reggae musician, chef and entrepreneur was approached at the World Food Market by a BBC researcher. An invitation to appear on the popular Dragons' Den programme soon followed, and with his family's support – and a little divine inspiration – Levi literally sang the praises of his homemade sauce (based on his grandmother's recipe), securing the backing of two Dragons along the way. One of these, Peter Jones, helped facilitate the almost overnight success of the sauce by immediately securing listings in Sainsbury's stores nationwide, practically unheard of for an unknown brand. Since then the phenomenal demand for

Reggae Reggae Sauce has resulted in sales of almost 1.8 million bottles, making a significant impact on the UK Caribbean food market. This sector has seen 52 per cent growth in sales in the last five years, and was estimated to be worth £41 million in 2007 (Source: Thai and Other Emerging Ethnic Foods – UK, Mintel 2007). The popularity of the sauce is further demonstrated by its recent infiltration into mainstream franchises such as Hungry Horse and Slug and Lettuce pubs (each now including a Reggae Reggae chicken burger on its menu) and, most recently, the newly launched Reggae Reggae Chicken Sub at Subway outlets.

Levi has used the success of his inaugural sauce as a springboard from which to build the Levi Roots brand, now comprising three core products: Reggae Reggae Sauce, Love Apple Tomato Ketchup and Fiery Guava Dipping Sauce. Using recipes handed down through generations, the products offer authenticity and versatility while also being an

easy introduction to Caribbean dishes. The original Reggae Reggae Sauce, for example, has a range of uses from marinade to condiment and during its short lifespan has already acquired cult culinary status. Love Apple Tomato Ketchup (also based on Levi's grandmother's recipe) blends Jamaican ingredients such as sun-ripened tomatoes with hot scotch bonnet chillies and allspice, making it a modern alternative to the traditional British condiment. Fiery Guava Dipping Sauce is a fruity blend of guava and scotch bonnet chillies.

As the face of the brand, Levi plays a key part in its promotional and marketing strategy; his laidback Jamaican cool and music credentials (as a MOBO nominated musician) appeal to a young target audience through regular TV and radio appearances, as well as widespread print and online media. With his life-story as colourful as the Caribbean cuisine he creates, Levi is a true ambassador for the brand combining his two key passions: music and food. These twin obsessions were first showcased back in 1991 through the 'Rasta'raunt', a food stall selling an array of foods (including Reggae Reggae Sauce) at London's Notting Hill Carnival.

The newly launched Reggae Reggae Cookbook enables consumers to recreate the vitality and flavours associated with Caribbean cooking in their own home. It offers 80 eclectic and easy-to-follow recipes such as Mash Up Eggs, Guinness Punch, and Sweet Potato

Pudding; from simple dishes for students to feasts for friends, all the recipes are accompanied by anecdotes in Levi's straight-talking style. Caribbean food is already proving a hit in the UK, due to its sweet taste and one-pot communal approach. A key long-term objective of Levi Roots' brand – in addition to extending its range of products – is to build on this popularity, taking a crucial step closer to its goal of becoming the number one brand in Caribbean cuisine in the UK.

ROUNDHOUSE

From modest Victorian beginnings – as a steam engine repair shed – to legendary cultural venue, the Roundhouse has an enviable heritage few are able to match.

roundhouse.org.uk

CoolBrands
2008/09

Photography: Sophie Laslett

Since playwright Arnold Wesker established Centre 42 at the Roundhouse in 1964 – the first time the building was used as an arts venue – it has played host to many seminal performances.

On 1st June 2006, the Grade II* listed north London landmark reopened following extensive refurbishment. This pivotal date in the venue's history was marked by an explosive new show, Fuerzabruta. It was the culmination of more than a decade's hard work, led by philanthropist Sir Torquil Norman.

The transformation was nothing short of remarkable. Architects John McAslan + Partners retained and restored many of the original features while, at the same time, creating a modern facility capable of accommodating and developing a long term international artistic programme. The Main Space, with a stunning glass lantern centrepiece (allowing natural light in for the first time since the 1860s), can house 1,800 people seated or 3,300 standing, allowing large-scale productions. Recent highlights include the annual BBC Electric Proms season, the Royal Shakespeare Company's Histories and Lucha Libre London.

The Roundhouse's artistic plans include circus, music festivals, large scale theatre, installations, talks and screenings but it is

the organisation's focus on young people that makes it a leader. The Roundhouse places young people at its heart, involving them at every level, from membership of the Board of Directors to generating marketing campaigns.

Throughout the year, the Roundhouse delivers creative projects for up to 6,000 13-25 year-olds from all backgrounds, covering radio, music production, drama, poetry, TV, sound engineering, photography, VJ skills and more. The professionally led projects cost just £2 and take place in the Roundhouse's 24 state-of-the-art studios that lie directly beneath the Main Space.

It is the interaction between the artists on stage and the young people that makes the Roundhouse unique. Young people have interviewed Sir Paul McCartney for the Roundhouse's online radio station during the BBC Electric Proms, taken musical advice from James Brown and worked with Apple to deliver a live stream of Underworld's Roundhouse performances to 50,000 people across the world. In this safe environment young people can develop

self-esteem and confidence or gain valuable experience to help launch a career.

For three months of every year the Roundhouse is available for hire for corporate and private events for anywhere between 200 and 2,000 guests. Yet even in this more conventional role it sticks to its guiding principles; all income goes directly towards the Roundhouse's work with young people. As a charity, it is also reliant upon corporate sponsorships and public and private funding to continue this work.

Since reopening, almost half a million people have attended an event at the Roundhouse. Its enviable musical heritage – the venue has previously played host to the likes of Jimi Hendrix and the Doors (their only UK gig) – has been revived, with performances from Kasabian, Jarvis Cocker, Paul McCartney, The Chemical Brothers, The Beastie Boys, The Who, Morrissey and James Brown.

As a pioneer of contemporary culture the Roundhouse has continually pushed boundaries. Today it offers diversity in music, theatre, dance and circus, in addition to nurturing young creative talent.

Photography: Will Pearson

S. PELLEGRINO

Bringing a touch of Italian tradition to tables across the world, from family to fine dining, S. Pellegrino is one of the world's most established bottled mineral waters.

sanpellegrino.com

The foothills of the Italian Alps provide the source of S. Pellegrino, a mineral water with a composition that has remained the same over hundreds of years.

The town of San Pellegrino, in the Lombardy region of northern Italy, has long been associated with natural health benefits. In 1839, it became a spa resort, building up a rejuvenating reputation that continues to attract visitors from all parts of the globe today. In 1899, the San Pellegrino Company was founded and began distributing what has since become one of the world's oldest and most established bottled mineral waters. More than 35,000 bottles were sold during S. Pellegrino's first year of production – 5,500 of those going overseas.

A key part of the enduring appeal of S. Pellegrino lies in its active ingredients: a combination of 14 minerals and natural trace elements. One litre of S. Pellegrino contains 20 per cent of the recommended daily amount of calcium and 16 per cent of the recommended amount of magnesium.

S. Pellegrino is an anti-uric mineral water with a composition that has remained unchanged since its first official analysis took place back in the late 1700s. It emerges from source at a constant temperature of 25-26 degrees, containing a distinct blend of elements – components that also make up the human body. A rare, perfect combination of dissolved minerals and natural CO_2 gives S. Pellegrino its pleasant, refreshing and lightly sparkling taste.

In 1932, Sanpellegrino Sparkling Fruit Beverages were first introduced. Relaunched in 2007, the drinks are available in Aranciata, Limonata and Chinotto variants.

While S. Pellegrino has been an inherent part of Italian lifestyle for more than a century, its appeal extends much further than its country of origin. It now exports to over 110 countries, with 75 per cent of total sales coming from overseas. In 1957 it added Acqua Panna to its portfolio of premium waters aimed at the fine dining market. Originating in the Tuscan hills, the still mineral water has a well-balanced chemical composition, which results in the smooth taste that makes Acqua Panna a key enhancement to the brand's 'Fine Dining Waters' offering.

Brand promotion of S. Pellegrino seeks to enhance its strong links to the art of choosing, cooking and eating good food. In 2007 it became the leading sponsor of the 'Oscars' of the gastronomy industry, The S. Pellegrino World's 50 Best Restaurants list, which is compiled by a selection of prominent food writers, critics, publishers and commentators. Now in its seventh year it has grown into an internationally influential event, globally recognised as a credible indicator of the best places to eat.

The S. Pellegrino Cooking Cup is an annual regatta held on the waterways of Venice, putting cooking and sailing skills to the test. The brand's involvement reinforces its connection with the Italian way of life by combining three leading Italian passions: food, classical architecture and sporting prowess. 2006 saw the first British entry in the event's six year history when Tom Aitkens, the youngest ever Michelin-starred British chef, climbed aboard to demonstrate his skills – collecting the award for 'Best International Chef' along the way. Angela Hartnett showcased her repertoire in 2007 and won the coveted title once again for the UK.

S. Pellegrino has strong brand values rooted in its Italian heritage: tradition, quality and authenticity. These, like its mineral water, continue to stand the test of time.

SAMSUNG

An innovative approach to design has been the guiding light for Samsung Electronics, morphing from small-scale manufacturer into one of the world's strongest and most powerful technology companies.

samsung.com/uk

From its South Korean origins The Samsung Group has grown into a global corporation operating worldwide across sectors as diverse as finance, chemicals and heavy industry.

The company, established in 1969, now employs around 150,000 people in 134 offices, across 62 countries. At the forefront of its recent growth is Samsung Electronics, currently one of the world's fastest growing global brands; its success largely attributed to its strength in three key areas: memory chips, liquid crystal displays (LCDs) and handheld telephones. It is currently market leader in both memory chips and LCDs, and number two globally in handheld telephones.

The Samsung brand is built around the core values of technology, design and innovation which has, in turn, fostered an association with premium, cutting-edge global brands such as Microsoft, Bang & Olufsen, adidas, Giorgio Armani, Twentieth Century Fox and Universal Music Group. All these alliances involve the development of joint products or use existing Samsung technology to complement partners' offerings. In March 2008, Samsung and adidas joined forces to launch the miCoach phone – the first true sports mobile – amid growing public awareness of the importance of a healthy lifestyle.

Through diverse sports sponsorship – ranging from Chelsea Football Club to the Samsung Super League, and including an international Running Festival – Samsung has built strong brand awareness as well as a reputation for excellence in corporate citizenship. A key sponsorship agreement with The Olympic Games, which it has sponsored since 1988, will run through to 2016, covering the 2012 London Olympics and is a key platform for demonstrating the brand's defining technology. Wireless Olympic Works (WOW), for instance, enables the real-time transmission of Olympic Games information to mobile phones. By supplying officials, athletes, staff, volunteers and visitors with fast and reliable communications tools, Samsung contributes to the success of the Games and supports its mission of fostering unity within the global community.

In October 2007 Samsung joined forces with the European Olympic Committee (EOC), investing one million euros in a 'Youth Anti-Obesity' programme for children. The programme, launched across 750 schools and clubs in five key European regions (Croatia, Denmark, Ireland, Italy and the UK), is aimed at encouraging more children to participate in sports.

Innovation lies at the heart of the Samsung brand with 2007's research and development investment – in 23 global research facilities – reaching almost $6.5 billion. Some 36,000 researchers at any given time ensure that Samsung remains at the cutting-edge of innovation, leading the digital convergence revolution. It has accrued an impressive number of world firsts including the first Blu-ray player; the world's smallest colour laser printer; the slimmest mobile phone (Samsung U100, 2008 edition); and the first 40Nano 32GB Nand flash. Samsung has also gained widespread industry recognition for innovation, scooping more than 100 influential design awards between 2006 and 2007, including 26 awarded by the prestigious International Forum Design (iF) organisation and four European Imaging and Sound Association (EISA) awards. The brand recently gained a further three '(inside) Design Excellence' awards (IDEAs) after being named 'Coolest International Brand of 2007' by Stuff Magazine.

Research and development, alongside cutting-edge product design, has yielded dramatic results for Samsung in recent years. However, its development has been supported and assisted by an aggressive marketing campaign. Six years ago Samsung made a pledge to re-position its brand, aligning itself with premium, cutting-edge products. The policy has paid off: according to an influential survey of the world's most valuable brands by BusinessWeek and Interbrand in 2007, Samsung ranks number 21, with a value of $16.85 billion (up from $3.2 billion in 1999) making it the most valuable consumer electronics brand in the world.

SHISEIDO

Combining tradition with innovation, Shiseido is a brand that epitomises understated, timeless elegance: pioneering science dedicated to a beautiful and artful way of living.

shiseido.co.uk

SHISEIDO

A contemporary appeal belies Shiseido's long history; it was in 1872 that founder Yushin Fukuhara set up Japan's first Western-style pharmacy, in Tokyo's upmarket shopping district, the Ginza.

Innovation has always been part of Shiseido's brand structure; launching Japan's first toothpaste in 1888, followed by Eudermine in 1897, a skin lotion so scientifically advanced that it is still being sold today, more than a hundred years later. During the first half of the 20th century Shiseido concentrated on the Japanese market. In 1957 it began trading overseas but it was only in 1980, through its collaboration with French artist Serge Lutens, that the brand's reputation began to take hold. As Shiseido's international image creator, Lutens successfully fused Eastern and Western artistic culture to create a global brand image that paved the way for Shiseido's UK launch, held at Harrods in 1987.

The characters that make up the brand name, Shiseido, come from an ancient Chinese phrase meaning 'praise the virtues of the earth, which nurtures new life and brings forth new values'. The distinctive name reflects the company ethos: a pioneer in combining Eastern aesthetics and sensibilities with Western

science and business practices – essentially blending tradition with technology.

Research and development are key to the brand. Expenditure in this area represents a substantial proportion of turnover with more than 1,000 dermatologists, biologists and researchers currently employed worldwide. There are 13 international Shiseido research centres that between them have patented more than 1,500 unique formulas. The centres operate across seven fields: basic research, life sciences, pharmaco-science, innovative products, pharmaceuticals, advanced skin research, and safety and

analysis; all focused on manufacturing products in keeping with the Shiseido brand ethos.

More than 130 years in the cosmetic industry, garnering extensive knowledge of skin physiology and aromachology, has given Shiseido advanced insight into beauty methods and practices. Both men and women's product lines are aimed at targeting individual needs using the most up-to-date technology available, while ensuring that every product is still suitable for use on the most sensitive skins.

Shiseido's skin care ranges are formulated to address a variety

of conditions and problems, from young skin to premature ageing and mature skin. At the heart of its offering lies The Skincare, a line aimed at strengthening the skin's own protective and restorative functions to resist stress and fight the early signs of ageing. The Benefiance, Bio-Performance and Future Solution ranges add further treatments to Shiseido's array of anti-ageing products. Pureness, meanwhile, is designed to address the problems specific to young skin, targeting blemishes, shine and enlarged pores as well as excess sebum and dehydration.

Shiseido's make-up range is continually evolving; developments such as Advanced Luminous Technology, a patented technology designed by the brand that allows the manipulation of colour and texture using light, mark it out as an industry innovator. Since March 2007, Dick Page has assumed the role of artistic director for Shiseido's global colour collection, Shiseido The Makeup. His renown as a make-up artist and experienced perspective bring an added dimension to the brand's market standing.

Shiseido has evolved from its Japanese roots into a global company. But, while products have advanced, the brand's principles remain virtually unchanged from the day it launched its first product. Shiseido seeks to lead the way in the advancement of skin care science and fashion-focused make-up collections, to contribute to a beautiful and artful way of living.

SPECIALIZED

Created by riders, for riders, Specialized may have a global distribution network but the company remains committed to its founding principle of making everyone's time on a bike that little bit better.

specialized.com

CoolBrands
2008/09

It takes passion and a belief in something to sell off nearly everything you own – including your treasured VW van. In 1974, Specialized's founder, Mike Sinyard, did exactly that.

Noting the enthusiasm Europeans had for both their high-tech bikes and equipment, Sinyard spotted a gap in the US market; the demand for bike technology existed but there were, at that time, very few products available. Cashing in most of what he owned in order to fund his new venture – providing high-end bicycle components and equipment to the US market – was a gamble that paid off. The decision to focus on top-of-the-range technology led to the company's name, which was adopted from the terminology used by riders when referring to the intricate components and parts that went into making up a racing bike. But even Sinyard had little idea that the brand would have such a major impact on the growth of the biking sector and accessibility to the sport.

Despite being in business for more than three decades, Specialized's founding principle – to focus on the riders' needs through technically advanced products – is even more valid today than when the brand was first conceived. Its roots

lie in innovation; the original Stumpjumper, built in 1981, led the way as the first mountain bike available for sale in local shops. Pre-Stumpjumper, riders had been limited to using road bikes on dirt free roads and smooth trails; the Stumpjumper pushed the limits of off-road possibilities.

Almost 35 years on from when the company was first founded, Specialized now has an extensive product range that reaches far beyond the machines themselves; from men and women's active clothes ranges to pumps, helmets, cutting-edge optics and ergonomically sculpted saddles – all designed with the same attention to detail and up-to-the-minute technology applied to its bikes.

Founded in Morgan Hill, California – where company headquarters still remain – Specialized is not only an industry leader in cycling technology but has also demonstrated its commitment to global cycling advocacy and environmental consciousness through initiatives such as its annual Bike to Work Day challenge, Recycle a Tyre project (which has seen more than four tons of bicycle tyres recycled to date), and the Specialized employee Commute Club, which, since it began in 2006, has offset more than 23 tons of CO_2 emissions through people switching from motorised forms of transport to cycling to work.

Specialized is as passionate about environmental issues as it is about technology. In 2007 it combined these

twin obsessions when it joined forces with Goodby Silverstein & Partners to launch the Innovate or Die Pedal-Powered Machine Contest. With additional support from Google Inc (by way of a specially created website), the competition challenged participants to create a pedal-powered solution for offsetting climate change. Eligible entrants were invited to post videos on YouTube to document each pedal-powered solution; winning entries were then selected by a panel of distinguished judges – including Specialized founder Mike Sinyard, Rich Silverstein from Goodby Silverstein & Partners and Google's director of climate change and energy initiatives, Dan Reicher – with prizes including US$5,000 cash and Specialized Globe bicycles. Globes, Specialized's premier 'vehicle for change', have also been put to work at Google's main Mountain View campus where 350 are currently in operation.

Over the years Specialized has picked up a host of awards

that recognise and value the contribution it has made to cycling, not only in the design and technological innovation of the bikes themselves, but also for the continuing creativity, drive and passion on which the brand has been built.

ST MARTINS LANE

St Martins Lane is an urban hotel with an original attitude.
Setting out to stimulate the senses, it aims to provide its guests
with a singularly magical and uniquely personal experience.

stmartinslane.com

With its daring disregard for convention, uncompromising attention to detail and personal service, St Martins Lane challenges the notion of what constitutes a hotel.

It was in 1999 that Morgans Hotel Group (pioneers of the 'boutique hotel' concept, which revolutionised the hospitality industry) first ventured into Europe, choosing for its opening gambit, St Martins Lane, a seven-storey, 204-room hotel at the heart of Covent Garden; a natural choice given London's cultural and artistic renaissance.

The Group's visionary founder Ian Schrager called upon the skills of design guru Philippe Starck (his cohort on many other landmark projects, such as Royalton and Hudson in New York, Delano in Miami Beach and LA's Mondrian) to challenge the frequently bland and formulaic UK hotel experience. The pair's goal was to create a distinct environment, devoid of the usual constraints and restrictions associated with corporate design; reinforcing the idea that modern luxury is less about monetary gain and more about creating new experiences, of being there and in the know.

One of St Martins Lane's most impressive design features is its lobby: the theatrical and social hub of the hotel. Eclectic furnishings and original touches mark a clear move away from previous hotel fads and trends, creating a moving set that reinforces the theatrical whimsy of the design. Fantasy and reality merge into one with the surrealist pairing of assorted items, such as oversized columns and angled alcoves painted a deep fluorescent yellow.

The lobby's Light Bar takes atmospheric, interactive lighting to new heights with a constantly shifting light installation visible through the acid-etched entry doors. Inside are four separate, colour-saturated niches; within each area, everything from the walls (hung with floor-to-ceiling close-up portraits by world-renowned French photographer Jean Baptiste Mondino) to the Starck-designed chrome chairs, is crafted in the same colour as the light within.

Light is also a key feature of the hotel's rooms; each has an interactive system (the first of its kind in a UK hotel) that enables guests to control their personal environment as they literally 'light their mood' from a custom-designed dial. At night, and from the outside, the differently coloured rooms create a mosaic of light.

Other room features include: a glowing onyx desktop, within-window Venetian blinds that work via a magnet, and mounted terracotta pots with pale pink begonias – a nod to traditional English gardens.

Under the direction of famed restaurateur Jeffrey Chodorow, the hotel has several eating spaces that include Asia de Cuba – offering a fusion of Asian and Latin cuisine – and the Rum Bar, a playful take on the traditional English pub, where guests are integrated into the overall design as they lean against bespoke Starck 'lean-on' tables, crafted to create interesting shapes and visual puns.

Asia de Cuba features a series of five colonnades running through the restaurant (each a creation in its own right), perhaps the most striking of which is the photography column, housing a collection of signed black and white photos by the likes of Malik Sidibe, Samuel Fosso, Cornelius Yao, August Azaglo and the late De Para. All installations are changed regularly, not only to showcase artists but so that guests – in line with the hotel's founding principles – will come to expect the unexpected.

STORM

Pioneering the careers of defining and diverse individuals,
Storm is a major player in an industry that has globalised
beyond recognition over the past 20 years.

stormmodels.com

Photography: Dusan Reljin

storm

Photography: Ben Watts

Photography: Nick Knight

Photography: Steven Meisel

Photography: Jo Metson Scott

As a brand, Storm's strength lies in its ability to combine the artistic and commercial elements of fashion in a way that appeals to both the industry and the public, effectively acting as a bridge between business and the consumer.

Storm's philosophy has always been to give the highest level of service possible – providing guidance and longevity to careers based on talent and achievement. In a highly competitive industry the most sought after models are those who offer something extra: Kate Moss, Lily Cole, Sophie Dahl, Cindy Crawford, Eva Herzigova, Carla Bruni, Monica Bellucci and Alek Wek are rightly acknowledged as stars whose talents reach beyond the camera's lens.

Founded by maverick model agent Sarah Doukas over 20 years ago, Storm became known for discovering a diverse and exciting range of faces. Sarah famously spotted a then 14 year-old Kate Moss, while waiting for a plane at JFK airport. Four years later Kate was contracted exclusively to Calvin Klein – an early landmark in a career that has set the standards to which many aspire.

Kate's achievements in the industry are legendary and her extensive portfolio of iconic work stands out. Long acknowledged as one of the world's style-icons, it was a natural progression for Kate to launch a fashion collection. Her partnership with retail giant Topshop has been exceptional and both her label – Kate Moss Topshop – and fragrance line, Kate Moss Parfums,

showcase an ability to understand the intricacies of an industry that is increasingly demanding, both creatively and commercially.

In 2005 Lily Cole was discovered by Storm in Covent Garden. The face of many prestige brands, Lily is now one of the most successful models in the world, and is further recognised for her consistent support of environmental issues. She has also enjoyed success as an actress with a debut role in 'St Trinian's', followed by leads in Terry Gilliam's 'The Imaginarium of Dr Parnassus' and Sally Potter's 'Rage' – both films released in 2009.

Model Jourdan Dunn, spotted in 2005 in Primark, has also made her mark as a model with integrity; the young star made her cover debut for Italian Vogue's July 2008 issue, shot by Steven Meisel, which set out to embrace black women in the modelling world. Already she is a name that people recognise and associate with an agency that celebrates diversity.

In 2006 Storm opened a Special Bookings division to offer representation to high-achievers from across the entertainment world. With its strong commercial relationships, Storm is well placed to build credible brand partnerships for its clients, including Emma Watson, Joe Calzaghe, The Queens of Noize, Riley Keogh, Peaches Geldof, Katherine Jenkins, Paolo Nutini and Rupert Everett.

Storm represents a diverse range of charismatic and iconic individuals for photographic, publicity, licensing and design projects. The strength of its reputation has been achieved through strategic and thoughtful career planning over two decades. Its success is synonymous with that of its clients. Storm remains at the forefront of fashion and youth culture, while endeavouring to set new standards based on its core principles of industry and integrity.

TANQUERAY

Recognised worldwide as the bartenders' choice, it is the 'taste of intensity' of Tanqueray® gin that lies at the very heart of its numerous drinks accolades.

tanqueraygin.com

CoolBrands
2008/09

It was in 1830 that Charles Tanqueray first established his distillery in Bloomsbury, London. Wanting to make the world's best gin, he set out to create the most distinctive, crisp, dry gin on the market.

His aim was to make a stylish and sophisticated gin that would be enjoyed by his friends, peers and those of impeccable taste, a vision of a world-class gin that continues to this day. The timeless recipe has been passed down through generations and remains a closely guarded secret, entrusted to just four people.

To ensure the smoothest of tastes, the spirit is distilled three times before botanicals are added for the fourth and final distillation, which means there is nothing to mask the aroma of the botanicals or cloud their taste. To deliver the intense taste unique to Tanqueray gin, only the finest botanicals are used, including juniper, coriander and angelica – just one in every 10 Tuscan juniper berries is deemed good enough for inclusion. By bottling the spirit at a higher ABV than most of its competitors, Tanqueray retains its unique flavour even after dilution, enabling it to deliver the perfect 'Tanqueray & Tonic'. All Tanqueray gin is now made at a single distillery,

at Cameronbridge, Scotland, ensuring consistent quality and balance of flavour.

Over the years Tanqueray has been favoured by style leaders; from allegedly being the drink of choice for Frank Sinatra and the Rat Pack, to consistently picking up accolades from awards juries the world over. In 2007, the makers of Tanqueray gin collected Double Gold Medals at the San Francisco World Spirits Competition for the fourth consecutive year, as well as the title of 'Best Gin in Show'.

Today, Tanqueray can be found in the finest hotels, bars and clubs around the world, catering for discerning individuals with distinctive tastes; a fact that has made Tanqueray the best-selling imported gin in the US, and means Tanqueray is now available in more than 140 international markets.

The brand received the ultimate seal of approval when, in two

independent global bartenders' surveys (conducted by Two Minds Research in 2006 and 2008) it was named as 'the bartenders' choice' of gin, an accolade which firmly endorses the distinctive taste of Tanqueray that cuts through mixers and produces world class cocktails. Tanqueray came first in the majority of categories including 'best tasting gin', 'best quality gin', 'best gin for cocktails', 'the gin seen in the very best bars', 'the gin [bartenders] would recommend to customers' and 'the gin with the most heritage'.

In keeping with the distinctive taste of Tanqueray, the bottle is also a clearly recognisable brand trait. Unchanged since 1948, the shape is based on a classic three-part cocktail shaker, while the distinctive 'T' seal on the front of the bottle continues to be seen as a guarantee of authenticity and quality, reminiscent of early Tanqueray production when the bottles were sealed with wax. The look is completed

with a pineapple on the bottle top; a feature of the Tanqueray family crest and universally recognised as a symbol of hospitality.

In today's crowded marketplace, Tanqueray stands out as a gin with substance as well as style, recognised by barmen and consumers alike.

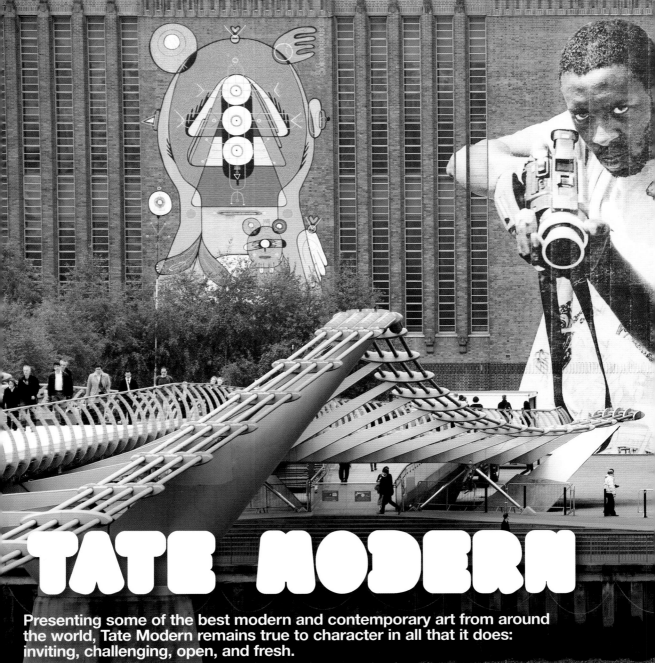

TATE MODERN

Presenting some of the best modern and contemporary art from around the world, Tate Modern remains true to character in all that it does: inviting, challenging, open, and fresh.

tate.org.uk

TATE

Part of the Tate family, and housed in an imposing former power station on the bank of the River Thames, Tate Modern is the most populated modern art gallery in the world.

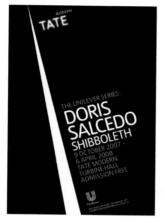

Major works by Picasso, Dalí and Warhol are exhibited in Tate Modern's free Collection, alongside current contemporary pieces, while recent blockbuster special exhibitions have included Rothko, Street Art and Doris Salcedo's Shibboleth – the huge crack ripping up the Turbine Hall as part of The Unilever Series.

Tate Modern runs a number of marketing campaigns each year. Although most are linked to the gallery's programme of exhibitions and events – by way of conventional, high profile press and advertising on the London Underground – it also experiments with more unusual techniques and strategies to attract different audiences. To promote 2008's Street Art exhibition, blank posters were produced and taken to skate parks where paints and spray cans were provided, allowing young people to create their own posters. One hundred of these bespoke posters were then displayed on commercial advertising sites across London. The aim of the initiative was to capture the mood of the Street Art exhibition in an engaging way, offering valuable exposure for the young adults' artwork, challenging them to do something with the art, rather than just telling them about the project.

Tate Modern was the first major gallery in the UK to brand itself – as part of the wider Tate brand – and continues to lead the field internationally in arts communication: intelligent, though not overly academic, and challenging but never intimidating.

Developed by world-renowned brand consultants Wolff Olins, the Tate brand encompasses Tate's four gallery sites – Britain, Modern, Liverpool and St Ives – and unites them through an ever-changing, four-faceted logotype. In a design that mirrors Tate's approach, a simply written 'TATE' is modelled to provide a range of logos that reflect the fluidity and dynamic nature of the brand. The four galleries, each with a distinct personality and specific offering, are linked by a single idea which aims to be both an invitation and a challenge, underpinning everything that Tate does: 'look again, think again'.

Tate's brand values are imbued, not just through art and in its own design, but also throughout every other aspect of the organisation. Its food subsidiary, Tate Catering, for example, aims to provide impeccably sourced and honestly priced produce, while Tate Modern Restaurant offers breathtaking views across London and a wine list chosen by sommelier Hamish Anderson. Tate Entertaining (its events company) runs both indoor and outdoor events that reinforce the brand mantra – inviting, challenging, open, and fresh. An exciting new event that takes place inside and outside Tate Modern is The Long Weekend, a four-day music and art extravaganza that takes place over the May bank holiday each year.

Tate has established a distinct brand appeal through its accessibility and a forward-thinking approach to art; a democratisation of gallery-going without the need to 'dumb down' and a shift of focus from art collections to the whole experience by putting people before art. At the forefront of its sector, Tate strives to step forth into uncharted territory.

THE CINNAMON CLUB

Challenging the notion that Indian cuisine can only be created using age-old recipes and ideas, The Cinnamon Club demonstrates how evolution and adaptation can create a new chapter in gourmet excellence.

cinnamonclub.com

THE CINNAMON CLUB

Housed in the Grade II listed former Westminster Library, a stone's throw from London's Westminster Abbey, The Cinnamon Club's neo-colonial feel fits perfectly with its distinctive style of Indian haute cuisine.

The reverential hush of 1893 (when the building opened as London's first public library) may have long since been replaced by the noisier sounds of diners, but much of the building's old world charm has been retained; parquet flooring, Indian marble imported from Rajasthan, and grand domed skylights that impart a sense of Victorian grandeur and occasion. Four separate areas make up The Cinnamon Club: a large dining room seating 130; a discreet and cosy mezzanine level overlooking the dining room; a 60-seat private dining room, with all the grandeur of the rest of the building; and a modern cocktail bar, neatly tucked away downstairs, with three projector screens showing Bollywood films, both classic and contemporary.

Run by managing director Rohit Chugh and executive chef Vivek Singh, The Cinnamon Club has, in recent years, established itself as a leading exponent of evolved modern Indian cuisine, through unique dishes such as smoked rack of lamb with Rajasthani corn sauce and pilau rice. Changing menus and a carefully selected wine list reflect the brand's cornerstones of innovation and creativity. The Cinnamon Club has also worked with two of France's leading winemakers, Michel Chapoutier and Gregory Patriat (of Jean-Claude Boisset), to produce the restaurant's own cuvées, ideally suited to its cuisine.

Since its launch, The Cinnamon Club's challenge has been to define Indian haute cuisine that, while inspired by traditional recipes, ingredients and cooking techniques, still takes advantage of modern European influences and local produce. The restaurant offers à la carte lunch and dinner menus – updated regularly to make the most of seasonal availability – as well as a gastronomic six-course tasting feast and breakfast and brunch menus, while special festival menus are run throughout the year.

The brand's commitment to quality extends to its two bars where trademark cocktails, such as the Cinnamon Bellini and Spiced Martini, display the same creative flair and attention-to-detail as its culinary concoctions. Bespoke drinks are also offered, including cardamom and cinnamon infused vodka and a special edition Cinnamon Club Glenlivet 1975 malt.

Brand marketing also focuses on an uncompromising commitment to quality, with intimate wine and spice dinners held in recent years to showcase the way in which specific wines and champagnes work well with Indian flavours. Brand extensions are similarly cuisine-led with its two cookbooks, The Cinnamon Club Cookbook and The Cinnamon Club Seafood Cookbook.

Since it opened in 2001, The Cinnamon Club has won praise, both for its inventive twists on old favourites and for rediscovering regional specialities. This culminated in its signature dish, roast saddle of Oisin red deer with pickling spices, being recognised in 2006 by Restaurant magazine as the 'Best Curry' in the annual UK Best Dishes Awards – an indication of the extent to which modern Indian cuisine is now accepted in its own right. A testament to its reputation, The Cinnamon Club has picked up a slew of additional awards over the past few years, including 'Best Classic Venue 2008' at the Theme Bar and Restaurant Awards and a commendation at the Spirits Business Scotch Whisky Masters 2008 for The Cinnamon Club Single Malt.

Building on its success, the next step for The Cinnamon Club is a new concept, Cinnamon Kitchen, due to launch in late 2008 in an imposing space in the heart of the City of London.

THE DESIGNERS REPUBLIC

Founded on Bastille Day 1986, The Designers Republic remains a declaration of independence – creative commercial thinking, freed from the shackles of received wisdom, conformity, compliance, consensus and complacency.

thedesignersrepublic.com

Your role as a
target market
explained

The Designers Republic (TDR) is on a mission: to liberate its collaborators' minds; to shine a light, showing them the way and helping them get there. Its message: communication by any means necessary.

Since it was established in 1986, TDR has set out to redefine design for the modern day, adhering to the 'Attitude > Approach > Art' formula. Standing for big ideas generated by thinking differently, for breaking the rules and for dissolving the traditional relationship between designer, client and audience, it is a formula that has delivered considerable commercial success. Yet TDR is driven not by commerce, but by a desire to break new ground, to go where no brand has gone before, and to take its clients with it.

As the name of its core strategy offering, Thinking and Doing™, suggests, TDR believes in taking an intelligent approach to its projects: visual communication is recognised as something that has the power to be a social and cultural archivist, an analyst and a cultural commentator; communication itself is seen not just as a

process, but as an achievement that must be realised through exploration rather than assumption; and belief systems – both real and deliberately imagined – are explored in the context of the individual, society and culture. It is a method designed to produce work that is honest and opinionated, original and inventive, and infused with logic.

Positioning itself as an 'ideas factory', TDR sees its clients not as a detached entity, but as like-minded people and collaborators. The benefit of such an approach is a flexible and workable solution for the client, built from shared knowledge that has been fine-tuned by specialist skills. It works towards creating a template for an adaptable, inclusive visual language that

any audience, be it client or consumer, can both understand and own.

In the years since its inception, TDR has sought out new ways to express new ideas to new audiences, from utilising motion graphics and digital, to sound and site-specific installations. Its own experiences as a brand – carving out a niche for itself as a design dissenter – have informed its ability to identify, understand and help solve problems for an enviable client list, which includes the likes of Coca-Cola, Orange, Sony, Warp Records, Nokia and Urban Splash.

Driven by a (self-confessed) low boredom threshold, TDR's business approach is to seek out interesting projects and partners; to choose to collaborate with those that celebrate the thinking and thrive on the doing; and to talk only to people who want to hear what it has to say, rather than those who want it to say what they want to hear. Crucially, it is a 'boredom' that is due to a restless spirit rather than a lack of commitment to creative problem solving.

TDR is built on a belief that the best design is intuitive, with the best designers those who are able to instinctively tap into diverse and shared cultural experiences. It considers research and thinking to be mirror methods, both demonstrating the accumulation and evaluation of new information, and it believes that the dialogue created should always inspire, inform, and entertain.

THE GLENLIVET

The definitive single malt whisky that put Scotland's best known whisky-producing region, Speyside on the map, The Glenlivet is 'the single malt that started it all'.

theglenlivet.com

CoolBrands
2008/09

Long before George Smith founded his Speyside distillery in 1824, the parish of Glenlivet already had a reputation for distilling whisky, albeit at that time illicitly.

The remote Speyside location meant that more than 200 illegal 'sma' stills' remained largely undisturbed for years, allowing the contraband whisky makers time to distil; the resulting smoother spirit, with its distinctive pineapple flavour, defined the enduring character of The Glenlivet and determined its label as 'the real stuff'.

As a native of Glenlivet the pioneering Smith tacitly understood the contribution its unique location (one of the most secluded glens in the Scottish Highlands) and high altitude made to the whisky's flavour. Once he was granted the first legal licence to brew in the area, his determination that 'only the best would do' saw him fend off aggressive competitors (in the form of smugglers) more than once, in the name of persevering and creating the Original Single Malt.

While other distillers attempted to cash in on the Glenlivet name (leading to it being labelled the 'longest glen in Scotland' due to so many whiskies claiming to originate there) the exclusive status of Smith's whisky was finally established in 1884, along with its right to be called The Glenlivet. Initially other distillers were able to include 'Glenlivet' in their title if it appeared after the name of the distillery, but even this compromise was short-lived and in 1888, as The Glenlivet's reputation soared, this speculative practice of 'quality by association' was ended by The Glenlivet trademark.

Today Smith's Original Single Malt has evolved into a definitive range of individual quality whiskies; while each retains its own distinctive character and style, all bear the unmistakable hallmark of The Glenlivet, a quality and consistency recognised through a host of industry accolades from the likes of the International Wine and Spirit Competition (IWSC) and the International Spirits Challenge (ISC). The Glenlivet Visitor Centre was also named 'Best Visitor Attraction' at the Whisky Magazine 2007 Icons of Whisky awards.

The brand's promotion in many countries is rooted in membership of a unique organisation, The Guardians. By becoming a 'Guardian of The Glenlivet' members benefit from a host of privileges that include exclusive tasting sessions, special events – such as a private tour of The Glenlivet Distillery and access to the 'hidden' library – and advance news about product offers and new bottlings. Once logged on, members also gain access to their own personal (and personally styled) homepage. As custodians of The Glenlivet's remarkable heritage, Guardians are uniquely placed to share the legacy of the Original Single Malt.

When George Smith opened his inaugural distillery he set a new industry standard, his whisky defining the taste of Speyside. From the classic appeal of The Glenlivet 12 Year Old through to the uncompromising integrity of the cask strength The Glenlivet Nadurra – a 16 Year Old single malt that reflects the unfettered and unspoilt spirit of the glen – and the exceptional expressions of 18, 21 and 25 Years Old, The Glenlivet is as fashionable today as it was in 1824.

THE WAPPING PROJECT

Celebrated for its singular combination of challenging contemporary art and performance, fine food and inspiring architecture, The Wapping Project is a melting pot of culture and cool.

thewappingproject.com

CoolBrands
2008/09

Photography: thomas zanon-larcher

W

Housed in Wapping Hydraulic Power Station on the north bank of the Thames, east of Tower Bridge, The Wapping Project opened to the public in October 2000.

Photography: Giada Bobbera, 2007

The Wapping Project is the creation of the distinguished theatre director, Jules Wright; its sense of drama is palpable. There is something essentially indefinable about The Wapping Project; it remains an idea in a state of transformation, consistently re-made and re-invented.

Wapping Hydraulic Power Station was built by the London Hydraulic Power Company in 1890. It harnessed Thames water to provide power to the surrounding docks and throughout the central London area. When it finally closed in 1977, it was the last of its kind in the world.

The conversion of Wapping Hydraulic Power Station for The Wapping Project was designed and conceived by architectural and design practice Shed 54. Rules were broken to give the contemporary elements a feeling of architectural impermanence – for example, stairs were made from mild steel and deliberately untreated so they would develop a patina of rust. The brand's visual identity was created by Vince Frost of Frost Design, and is a woodcut especially created to bring together the contemporary and raw elements which signify The Wapping Project. The font was made by taking moulds from the text on the original machinery and is used on all printed material.

The juxtaposition of the light and transparent qualities of the new with the gravity of the original building intensifies the effect of each. The new architecture identifies with the beauty of the historic building and aims, above all, to create a backdrop against which artists can create audacious contemporary work.

The space also effortlessly incorporates the award-winning restaurant Wapping Food, which spills through the Engine and Turbine Houses. The restaurant is fuelled by the same sense of perfection and ambition, and Wright views the commissioning of the chefs in much the same way as she does the artists with whom she works. A daily changing menu, in-house butchery and carefully sourced produce have consistently marked out Wapping Food and defined its place within London's most serious restaurants. There are no obvious boundaries between the restaurant and the artistic programme, which is applauded internationally for its quirky curatorial position.

The body of work produced by The Wapping Project is the product of 20 years' experience and an unchallenged record of commissioning artists who have become major players in the UK's cultural landscape. All work in Wapping Hydraulic Power Station is site-specific and specially commissioned. Recent work includes 2007's Stairway by Shed 54 (pictured left), Bloom by Sam Spenser (pictured above), and Beware by Richard Wilson – all commissioned by The Wapping Project on behalf of Veuve Clicquot. Earlier benchmarks include All About Chairs, a series of 33 photography and choreography commissions (July-October 2003); Richard Wilson's Butterfly (spring 2003); NYC, the groundbreaking photography show of Magnum photographers and their work on New York (summer 2002); Elina Brotherus' Spring photography and video installation (winter 2001); Solo jazz performances for Jerwood: Solo With Light (winter 2001); Keith Haring's The Ten Commandments (summer 2001); Jerwood: Stairworks 10x8, an extensive choreography series on the external stairwell (summer 2001); Conductor by Jane Prophet (winter 2000); and Anya Gallaccio's Intensities and Surfaces, a 34 tonne ice-block commissioned for the derelict building in 1996.

So what is The Wapping Project? It's an idea rooted in a magical building and realised within it. While solid and substantial, it is also mercurial and inexplicable. It's where culture and cool mix.

THE ZETTER

A destination for those seeking style, superior service and value with a generous helping of fun, The Zetter is Clerkenwell's much-admired 'small hotel with a big personality'.

thezetter.com

The Zetter Hotel

Opening to wide acclaim in 2004, The Zetter set out to achieve style and character – without the aloof service and hefty price tag seen as typical of the London 'design hotel' scene.

The brainchild of restaurateurs Michael Benyan and Mark Sainsbury, The Zetter turned the London hotel market on its head with its reinterpretation of the 'boutique hotel' concept. Four years down the line, The Zetter's enduring popularity is evidence enough of its winning formula.

Michael and Mark first joined forces to help open the highly regarded Moro restaurant in Clerkenwell, alongside Sam and Sam Clark. A resounding success, the up-and-running restaurant left room for a new project in the pair's schedule and inspiration struck in the form of a magazine article featuring The Ace Hotel in Seattle. Impressed by its quirky warehouse renovation, Michael and Mark set about searching for a London location in which to realise their new hotel vision; a destination that both locals and visitors alike would be attracted to, offering personality as well as affordable style. Passionate about Clerkenwell, it was the obvious choice for these first time hoteliers and in the summer of 2001 they bought the Zetter building: a 19th century, five-storey warehouse, formerly home to the Zetter football pools.

Working with local architects, Chetwood Associates, innovation, sustainability and an environmental conscience were at the heart of all decision-making. Sustainable materials, eco-friendly paint and energy saving lighting have been used as standard, alongside groundbreaking features such as a state-of-the-art energy exchange system. The air conditioning system, meanwhile, uses water pumped from The Zetter's own 1,500-foot bore-hole

beneath the building, which is also the source of the restaurant's bottled spring water – continuing a Clerkenwell tradition that dates back to the 17th century when the area was famed for the health promoting qualities of its many springs.

To help translate The Zetter concept into reality, interior designers Precious McBane joined the project, with a brief to steer clear of the 'I could be anywhere' generic hotel experience. The Zetter was to provide its guests with a strong sense of place, marrying the original fabric of the building with a contemporary, yet quintessentially English, use of pattern and textiles. To reproduce the strong identity graphically, Michael and Mark turned to Fabian Monheim of Fly Productions. Bowled over by the wit and personality of his designs, they enlisted him to bring an illustrative sense of fun to even the smallest elements of the hotel, from laundry bags and matchboxes to blankets and water bottles.

At the heart of the hotel lies The Zetter Restaurant. Open and inviting, the restaurant has been instrumental in cementing the vision of The Zetter as a destination with appeal that extends beyond its hotel guests. A dynamically structured space, the restaurant encircles the ground floor and features giant sash windows that flood the space with light and look out over the cobbles of St John's Square. The Zetter is not style over substance, however, as it is the refreshingly friendly and approachable service that really makes it stand out from the crowd. The staff, led by general manager Justin Pinchbeck, are encouraged to bring their own personality and good humour to their role, creating the warm atmosphere that has been integral to The Zetter's success.

Following universal acclaim, a number of European Design awards and too few rooms to meet demand, it will only be a matter of time before another 'small hotel with a big personality' is added to The Zetter group.

TOP TRUMPS

Perennial favourite Top Trumps has reinvented itself as a game for the 21st century through combining nostalgia with new technology.

toptrumps.com

CoolBrands
2008/09

Top Trumps is a timeless classic that has, in recent years, tapped into the trend for retro games, acquiring a new generation of fans along the way.

The brand's reinvention began in the 1990s with Hasbro's buyout of games company Waddingtons. Along with well-known favourites Monopoly and Cluedo came an almost forgotten card game, Top Trumps. Games experts, Winning Moves bought the brand and, under the watchful eye of brand guardian Tom Liddell, Top Trumps was transformed into a slick, modern and profitable commodity.

The cards received a more sophisticated redesign with a new flip-top plastic case replacing its easily shattered predecessor, and where previously the game's core market had been 10 year-old boys, the new range was designed to appeal to all ages and both genders. Winning Moves also secured some heavyweight licensing deals, allowing Top Trumps to tap into the world of movies, celebrities and entertainment, alongside its existing sports cars, warships and jets.

One recent development is the first Collectors Edition, '45 Years of Time Travel', which comes in distinctive 'Tardis' packaging and features the first eight incarnations of

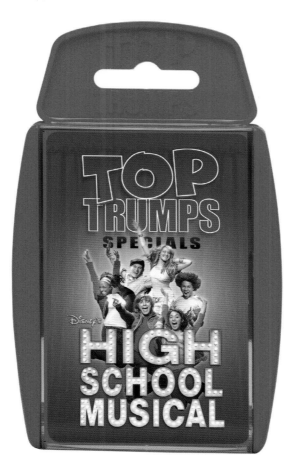

Doctor Who, his assistants and some of his deadliest enemies. Other titles launched in 2008 include: 'Hannah Montana', featuring Disney's schoolgirl pop diva; 'Ben 10' the boy superhero who transforms himself into alien beings; and the Star Wars pack, 'The Clone Wars'. New Classics titles include 'Gumball 3000 Custom Cars' and 'Ancient Egypt: Tutankhamun and the Golden Age of the Pharaohs'.

The last 12 months have also seen developments in the digital world of Top Trumps, as the brand launched into the video games arena with the very first Doctor Who game on Nintendo DS, Nintendo Wii, PlayStation 2 and PC in May 2008. Top Trumps can now be experienced on all of the major games consoles, as well as on mobile phones and interactive DVD – which allows players of the Bratz video game, for

example, to 'unlock' an embedded Top Trumps game if a certain level is exceeded.

The rollout of Top Trumps Live! – the brand's online game – has seen Top Trumps games created for Lucasfilm in San Francisco, as well as the NBA and Nickelodeon in New York, resulting in millions of Top Trumps games being played online each year.

Recently the Top Trumps brand has been used as a powerful, fun method of promoting the services and products of unrelated companies. In 2007, for instance, Winning Moves was commissioned by Sky News to create 'Politicos', an exclusive pack featuring some of the House of Commons' best-known characters. The coveted packs became the talk of the Party Political Conferences, receiving wide national press and online coverage. This kind of targeted activity and media presence helps to maintain a high-profile brand awareness.

The last two years have also seen Top Trumps used, with great success, as a consumer promotion by The Sun, the UK's biggest selling newspaper, by Paramount in the US and Canada, and by McDonald's Happy Meals across Europe.

Today Top Trumps is available in many formats, across Australasia, Japan, North America, the Middle East, and Europe; enjoyed as much by today's generation as the last.

URBAN SPLASH

Urban Splash has earned a reputation as one of the country's leading regeneration companies, delivering its mixed-use schemes through a combination of visionary, environmentally responsible design and entrepreneurial know-how.

urbansplash.co.uk

CoolBrands
2008/09

urbansplash

From niche northern developer to one of the UK's leading regeneration specialists, Urban Splash has just entered the third phase of its maverick journey.

Photography: Joakim Boren

The story began back in 1993, when Tom Bloxham and Jonathan Falkingham set up the company based on the founding principle of quality, sustainable design. Having already created a bar (just off Bold Street in Liverpool) the pair moved a short way to Concert Square for the inaugural Urban Splash project – providing the first loft-style apartments in the North-west. It was a sign of things to come: thought-provoking urban regeneration of dwindling city centres.

During its first 10 years Urban Splash concentrated its efforts on familiar territory; reviving one-time landmark buildings in Manchester and Liverpool. Through offering bespoke brochures and show flats – something no other developer was doing at that time – it was able to generate interest in areas and buildings that no-one else would touch.

In 2003 (and now worth around £7 million) Urban Splash won its first project outside the North-west, Royal William Yard in Plymouth, and set up a regional base in the area. By 2008 further regional offices had been established

in Liverpool, Birmingham and Bradford to oversee multi-million pound projects stretching the length and breadth of the county, from Plymouth to Morecambe and Glastonbury to Irvine. As the scope of its developments increased so too did staff numbers, from around 65 in 2003 to 274 in 2007, emulating the company's rapidly expanding portfolio. With its strong team ethos, Urban Splash is unique in the often cut-and-thrust world of developing; while creating a working environment for staff that fosters responsibility and

rewards endeavour, it also believes that workplaces should be relaxed and fun.

The brand's tongue-in-cheek humour is evident through its literature and website, an upbeat approach untypical of development strategists. Since the outset, Urban Splash has had an in-house graphics team that has set trends in marketing residential property in the UK. This creative entrepreneurial trait is evident in the brand's overall approach to business: it never promotes or advertises but lets its achievements speak for itself. The Urban Splash

philosophy is that great design needs no introduction.

Since the company was launched, awards have been an ongoing endorsement of the business, conveying support and confidence in its schemes, not only from potential buyers, partners and industry mentors but also, crucially, from the community. To date, Urban Splash has received 257 awards; 41 from the Royal Institute of British Architects, the most accrued by a single developer.

Working in partnership with councils and local communities is key to the company agenda. With Tutti Frutti, for example, (a street of homes designed and built by its owners and part of New Islington, Manchester's 29-acre Millennium Community) Urban Splash may be the lead developer in delivering the 1,700 new homes, office space, new canal, school and health centre, but it works in partnership with Manchester City Council, English Partnerships and Manchester Methodist Housing Association.

With more than £1 billion of work in progress and the creation of Urban Splash Hotels – to operate the newly opened Art Deco Midland Hotel in Morecambe – the brand's future, in keeping with its past, is to continue working with world class architects to produce world class, mixed-use buildings in an environmentally responsible way. Its privileged position as a private company enables it to think and invest in long term returns – essentially what good regeneration is all about.

Photography: Dan Hopkinson

VITRA

Since making a name for itself in 1957, producing furniture designed by Charles and Ray Eames, Vitra is today recognised for its innovation and diversity: from cultural initiatives to experiential architecture and design.

vitra.com

vitra.

While Charles and Ray Eames' work has left an enduring impression on Vitra, the company embraces new designers that exhibit exceptional creative skill and individuality through their work.

Vitra Edition is one such example; first launched in 1987, it acts as a laboratory for architects and designers to create experimental furniture and interior installations, without market or production constraints. With no existing collectors' market, it was a pioneering concept from the outset and the show's opening year featured seating designs by the likes of Frank Gehry, Denis Santachiara, Gaetano Pesce, Richard Artschwager, Ron Arad, Shiro Kuramata, Ettore Sottsass and Scott Burton. In the years that followed, Vitra Edition grew, establishing new designer relationships with contributions from Jasper Morrison, Alessandro Mendini, Borek Sipek and Philippe Starck. Vitra Edition not only creates diverse experimental pieces of contemporary design, available to collectors as a limited edition, but also contributes to the brand's ongoing design research.

Vitra's commitment to innovation and artistic exploration is not limited to individual pieces, however, with the Vitra Campus the jewel in its forward-thinking crown. A collection of signature architecture in Weil am Rhein, the Campus was conceived in 1981 following a major fire at the company's production base, which destroyed over half of the site's original capacity. When faced with the choice of a like-for-like prefabricated structure or an architecturally ambitious building, Vitra chose the latter, hiring British architects Nicholas Grimshaw to plan the rebuild. From the angular form of the Fire Station by Anglo-Iraqi architect Zaha Hadid, to the latest projects by Japan's Kazuyo Sejima and Ryue Nishizawa, or the Swiss Jacques Herzog and Pierre de Meuron,

over the years major world architects have been instrumental in transforming the one-time farmland into a site dedicated to experimentation and excellence.

The Campus is home to one of Vitra's most famous brand extensions, the Vitra Design Museum. It was in the early 1980s that CEO Rolf Fehlbaum (son of founder Willi Fehlbaum) began his collection of pieces by designers influential in the company's development; names such as Charles and Ray Eames, George Nelson, Alvar Aalto and Jean Prouvé. As his collection grew, so too did his desire for an architectural venue in which to house it. In 1987 he approached Frank Gehry about the building's design; the opening on 3rd November 1989 marked the completion of Gehry's first major European project.

Today, the Vitra Design Museum is internationally recognised as one of the world's most influential cultural institutions for research on design and architecture, producing its own exhibition catalogues that, thanks to contributions from renowned writers and photographers, have become industry standards, examining the cultural, historical and social significance of furniture design.

Vitra thrives on the diversity and scope of its remit. From the Vitra Campus to Vitra Edition, its work is based on an underlying conviction that everyday life is inspirational. One of Vitra's founding beliefs is that the design, development and use of the spaces in which people live and work benefits from a flexible approach, effectively through removing as many conventional boundaries as possible. Convinced that rooms and design can influence motivation, performance and health, it has set out to develop furniture and furnishing systems that do just that, while, at the same time, offering comfort, safety and support.

A project driven by a desire and determination to design the world, Vitra has set out to enrich everyday life through its products, architecture and collections.

wagamama

Democratic eating is at the heart of wagamama's philosophy; a combination of fresh, nutritious food in an elegant, communal setting that offers exceptional value for money.

wagamama.com

wagamama

The date: 1992. The setting: London's Bloomsbury. The concept: democratic eating. Modelled on Japan's popular ramen shops, wagamama introduced the notion of noodles as healthy, fast food to the UK.

From the outset, canteen style eating – long wooden communal benches – has been one of wagamama's distinctive brand signatures, as is its unique fusion of technology with customer service; each order is entered into an electronic handheld PC and zapped straight to the kitchen, enabling dishes to be served to order. No fuss and no delays, all just part of the wagamama service; you don't need a lot of money or extravagant surroundings to dine well.

A founding ingredient of wagamama's is ramen: big bowls of noodles in soup with vegetables, fish or griddle-cooked meat – essentially a nutritionally complete meal in a bowl. Other key dishes include stir-fried noodles and rice-based options as well as salads and desserts. In keeping with its egalitarian ethos wagamama does not separate starters from mains, offering instead a variety of side dishes such as meat and vegetable dumplings, skewered chicken, edamame and raw salads to accompany meals.

The Heathrow Terminal 5 restaurant, which opened in the spring of 2008, marked a double first for the brand: its first UK airport site and the first ever UK breakfast menu, launched to meet the needs of early morning travellers. From pan-Asian breakfast dishes to the more traditional English style, albeit with a definitive wagamama twist, the menu offered is diverse, and although currently exclusive to Terminal 5, plans to roll it out at additional selected sites are currently being considered.

wagamama's most effective form of promotion is the 'wagamama experience' itself. Mainly by way of word-of-mouth recommendation, it has accrued (and been short-listed for) a host of prestigious awards that reflect its enduring appeal. 2008 accolades include 'International Restaurateur of the Year' at the 2008 Global Retail & Leisure International Awards, 'Best Company' at the Retailers' Retailer of the Year Awards and Zagat's 'Most Popular London Restaurant', for the third year running.

Outside advertising, primarily to direct customers to its restaurants, and new media – in the form of the brand's vibrant website that changes almost daily – are also used to communicate offers, promotions and menu changes. Customers are encouraged to become wagamama online members so that alerts can be sent via email with news and rewards for their

loyalty. Over the years wagamama has also forged various partnerships with brands that have similar audience demographics, reaching additional membership bases through joint promotions.

Since 2004, wagamama's award-winning cookbooks, by acclaimed food writer Hugo Arnold, have enabled customers to recreate simple signature dishes in the comfort of their own kitchens by demonstrating the simplicity of the brand's food. But the unique wagamama message is never more evident than in the restaurants themselves. The fundamental aim is to create a combined positive experience – through its food, people and environment. wagamama works hard to be in tune with customer needs and strives to run its restaurants to the highest standards possible. Energy, a positive attitude and enthusiasm are an essential pre-requisite for all staff.

In the 16 years since its inception, wagamama has opened more than 90 restaurants worldwide. However close to home or far-flung the location – Europe, the Pacific Rim, the Middle East, the US and, most recently, Heathrow's Terminal 5 – the brand remains committed to ensuring customers receive the same experience; a culinary democracy where families, business professionals, backpackers, students and 'ladies who lunch' can discover its unique experience: positive eating + positive living.

WILLIAMS F1

In a sporting universe now dominated by large corporations,
Williams F1 has for three decades remained faithful to its founding
intention, to exist independently and to exist purely to race.

williamsf1.com

The most enduring partnership in Formula One, between Frank Williams and Patrick Head, dates back to 1978 when a team of just 17 debuted its inaugural car, the FW06, at the Argentine Grand Prix.

Today, the 500-man company has changed beyond recognition, but has nevertheless not deviated from its purity of purpose – to race and race alone. The brand's eventful 30-year history is punctuated with milestones, from its debut victory at Silverstone in 1979, to its first Constructors' and Drivers' World Championship just 12 months later.

Over the last 30 years Williams F1 has helped to make many companies famous, adding richness and depth to a variety of brands and helping a range of motor manufacturers enjoy success as Formula One World Champions, including Renault, Honda and Ford. A new chapter in the team's history began in 2006 when, retaining its characteristic independence from corporate ownership, it secured a multi-year engine agreement with Toyota and new title sponsorship with telecommunications giant AT&T.

Williams is run by racing purists; promotion of the corporate brand is deliberately low-key, with the Williams name standing behind the brands it is charged to promote. To a large extent the Williams brand is defined by the company it keeps. The team's commercial partners contribute to its overall look, tone, feel and values, believing it to be the best platform for promoting global brand awareness and forging effective business relationships.

With 18 races, spanning an eight-month season from March to November, Formula One has the largest TV audience of any annual global sport, 597 million unique viewers and more than 1.5 million minutes of coverage every year. This audience has witnessed the Williams team's 16 World Championships; 295 podium finishes, 113 victories (of which 33 have been one-two victories), 24 consecutive poles and a record 15 pole positions, out of a possible 16, secured in a single season two years in succession (1992-93) – a record equalled only by McLaren.

Williams' achievements are not limited to the track, however. Team Principal Frank Williams, the longest serving Team Principal in the sport, is also the only team boss to have received a knighthood, in addition to his 1986 CBE.

Redefining the brand for the company's fourth decade, the recently evolved Williams logo has three main aims: to represent a family business with Sir Frank Williams at its head; to reflect a solid and dependable engineering ethos, representative of the team's automotive roots; and to engender pride in every employee, from security guard to F1 driver.

Spending more than £100 million annually, building and racing six cars – for fun – demonstrates a pioneering spirit rarely seen in today's highly marketed world. Williams values technological innovation and independence more highly than commercial acceptance. Management processes are defined to facilitate instant, devolved decision-making while operations focus on research and development.

Williams defends its independence fiercely, competing against better-funded organisations. While the team competes in the spirit of sporting endeavour, it understands it has a vital role to deliver a return to its stakeholders and it is this, allied to a burning desire to win, that has driven Williams F1 to become one of the most successful sporting brands in the world.

YAUATCHA

Chinese tradition dictates that drink should not be served without food. Yauatcha, London's first all day dim sum restaurant and teahouse, offers a contemporary setting for eating, drinking and socialising – the traditional Chinese way.

yauatcha.com

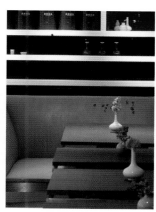

Taking inspiration from the colloquial Chinese saying 'yum cha', meaning to have tea, Alan Yau – the force behind Michelin-starred restaurant Hakkasan – opened Yauatcha in 2004.

By combining the custom and art of drinking tea with the social ritual of catching up with friends over food, Yauatcha offers value for money, mid market dining; an all day grazing experience with modern, authentic dim sum, cake and tea.

Yauatcha epitomises Yau's signature approach: marrying quality cuisine with cutting-edge design. As with his two other London eating establishments – Hakkasan and Busaba Eathai – Yau employed acclaimed designer Christian Liaigre to deliver its high-end contemporary look. Housed over two floors in the award-winning Richard Rogers Ingeni building in Soho, its two distinct areas are united by the design detailing that runs throughout; from the furnishings, lights and menu to the disposable chopsticks in flowered paper wrappers and pale green china cups and bowls.

The ground floor tea room comes complete with white marble and a full-height fish tank; a light and airy setting for afternoon tea, with a selection of petit gateaux and 150 varieties of tea. Distinctive East-meets-West flavour combinations, such as blue and black tea macaroons and matcha tea chocolates, typify the offering.

Downstairs in the cavern-like basement, 24 types of dim sum are on the menu, served from bamboo baskets and plates rather than the more conventional trolleys. Illuminated by electronic 'candles' and fibre optic 'stars', diners can glimpse the chefs at work behind a blue tinted glass screen. The menu is prepared under the strict supervision of head dim sum chef Soon Wah Cheong whose high standards have been recognised by influential industry

bodies such as Zagat and at the Möet Restaurant Awards. Yauatcha gained almost instant critical acclaim by receiving a Michelin star within a year of opening, emulating its sister restaurant Hakkasan: the only two Chinese restaurants in Europe to currently have Michelin recognition.

Yauatcha is currently working on further developing its teahouse retail offering with a range of incense, soaps and chinaware as well as chocolates, truffles, petit gateaux and patisseries. Specially designed packaging is used for takeaway cakes and patisseries, a brand attention to detail that extends to all of its merchandising. Yauatcha's range of candles, for example – made entirely from beeswax, so smokeless and paraffin free – was two years in development before being launched in March 2007, while the first range of china created specifically for use at the restaurant was a Japanese tea set by renowned Japanese designer Shin Azumi. Hsiao Fang, an accomplished Chinese potter, later designed a

series of Chinese tea sets and there are plans for Indian and English versions to follow, again by designers specially commissioned for Yauatcha.

Items are also available to buy online, through Yauatcha's newly launched website. Based on the premise of a love story and designed by creative publishers Tank, the website features a series of short films which explore the Yauatcha experience.

By taking one of the great etiquette-free grazing experiences – alongside sushi, tapas and meze – out of the context of the ordinary Chinese menu, Yauatcha has made dim sum accessible; a stylish introduction to the art of Eastern cuisine. The restaurant showcases Yau's talent for combining familiar elements of Chinese cuisine with the exotic of the Orient and contemporary chic. With expansion plans already underway to take the brand to its spiritual home, China, Yauatcha looks set to continue spreading the 'yum cha' word.

AUTHENTICITY ORIGINALITY INNOVATION

DESIRABILITY UNIQUENESS STYLE

COOLBRANDS 2008/09 THE RESULTS

STEPHEN CHELIOTIS

**Chief Executive, The Centre
for Brand Analysis & Chairman
of the Expert Council**

CoolBrands
2008/09

KEEPING YOUR COOL

When analysing last year's CoolBrands results, one of the first things I noted was that many of the top performers were not 'new kids on the block'; they were not brands that had sprung up from nowhere, a flash in the pan or a fad. In many cases they were highly established brands with a heritage dating back decades, or in some cases, more than a century. This confirmed that 'cool' is not necessarily a fleeting quality that cannot be retained; at least according to the experts and consumers surveyed during the research process.

In examining the 2008/09 results, this view has been reaffirmed. Not only are many of the strongest performers major players with a solid history, many of them have maintained their 2007/08 ranking. In fact a staggering 14 of last year's top 20 remain within it this year. Reviewing all of the CoolBrands results since the first survey in 2001, it is clear that many of these brands have consistently placed towards the top of the rankings. Furthermore, the gap between top brands and their competitors is often momentous; for example Agent Provocateur in eighth place is 100 places ahead of its nearest competitor, La Perla, while carrier Virgin Atlantic is 60 places ahead of the nearest transport company and 161 places ahead of its nearest direct rival in the airline sector, Singapore Airlines.

The brands that have dropped out of the top 20 this year are iPod, eBay, Green & Black's, iTunes, Prada and Amazon.co.uk.

There was a significant change in the definition and methodology for surveying and selecting the 2006/07 CoolBrands, but compare the results from the last three years (all of which were generated by the new methodology) and it is clear that certain brands are consistently outperforming the rest.

The best case in point is the number one brand, Aston Martin. Remarkably, the luxury car marque has topped the list for the last three years. If we think about the six core

factors that both the experts and consumers keep in mind when judging the brands – style, innovation, originality, authenticity, desirability and uniqueness – it is clear that the brand performs strongly on all counts.

With almost half of the Expert Council new to the process this year and an entirely different set of consumers taking part in the vote, it is incredible that out of the thousands of brands considered Aston Martin yet again rises to the top. It is even more remarkable when you consider that the brand does not undertake significant mainstream marketing or advertising campaigns. The brand's relationship with the James Bond films, it's only consumer-facing activity of note, undoubtedly has a positive effect that reaffirms the brand's stylish and innovative nature, but it would be wrong to assume that this alone is the key driver for the brand's ongoing success.

Aside from Aston Martin, brands maintaining their position in the top 20 are Apple, Bang & Olufsen, YouTube, Google, Nintendo, Agent Provocateur, Rolex, Tate Modern, Virgin Atlantic, Ferrari, Ducati, PlayStation and Lamborghini. In true CoolBrands fashion, this collection represents an interesting and eclectic mix of brands. Exclusive, luxury brands such as Rolex share the top 20 with democratic brands such as YouTube, while culture icon Tate Modern sits alongside brands that are arguably from the other end of the cultural spectrum, such as the games consoles Nintendo and PlayStation.

Whether these brands really are the most stylish, innovative and original leaders in their field is open to debate but, nevertheless, the perception that people have – both experts and consumers alike – is that they are the clear market leaders. This often stems from the initial impact the brand has on the category, which can remain powerful in people's minds. This is evident from the fact that 16 of this year's category winners – there are 35 categories in total – were also top of their sector last year.

Outside of the top 20, big category out-performers include: Storm beating its closest rival, Select Model Management, by 158 places;

1/Style
2/Innovation
3/Originality
4/Authenticity
5/Desirability
6/Uniqueness

COOLBRANDS 2008/09 TOP 20

RANK	BRAND	CATEGORY	MOVEMENT
1	Aston Martin	Automotive – Cars	none
2	iPhone	Technology – Telecommunications	new entry
3	Apple	Technology – General	+4
4	Bang & Olufsen	Technology – General	none
5	YouTube	Online	-2
6	Google	Online	-1
7	Nintendo	Leisure & Entertainment – Games & Toys	+2
8	Agent Provocateur	Fashion – Lingerie	none
9	Rolex	Fashion – Accessories, Jewellery & Watches	+5
10	Tate Modern	Leisure & Entertainment – UK Attractions & The Arts	+5
11	Dom Perignon	Drinks – Champagne	+20
12	Virgin Atlantic	Travel – General	-2
13	Ferrari	Automotive – Cars	-2
14	Ducati	Automotive – Motorbikes	-2
15	PlayStation	Leisure & Entertainment – Games & Toys	-9
16	Sony	Technology – General	+10
17	Nike	Sportswear & Equipment	+46
18	Bose	Technology – General	+10
19	Facebook	Online	new entry
20	Lamborghini	Automotive – Cars	-3

Expedia.co.uk trouncing closest competitor Trailfinders by 125 positions; Skype beating nearest telecom company O2 by 94 places; and innocent beating the next non-alcoholic drinks brand, Evian, by 50 places.

Other categories witness closer battles. Top hotel Malmaison, for instance, pips The Hoxton Hotel to the top spot by just one place. In the competitive footwear market, Manolo Blahnik beats Jimmy Choo by four places, reversing 2007/08's running order.

Returning to the battle within the top 20 itself, the fight of the games consoles reveals seventh place Nintendo leapfrogging 15th place PlayStation, reaffirming suggestions by the sales figures that Sony is losing that particular fight. The biggest riser within the top 20 is the iconic sportswear company Nike, having climbed 46 places since the 2007/08 rankings to reach 17th position. Another big riser, Dom Perignon jumps 20 places to finish just outside of the top 10 in 11th place.

Two new entries to the top 20, Facebook and iPhone, were not even in the 2007/08 top 500. This shows that despite my assertions that the top CoolBrands generally have an element of heritage, fresh-faced brands are not precluded from quickly presenting themselves as challengers for the top spots. But it is the ability to maintain this edge that is the real challenge. MySpace, Facebook's fellow social networking brand, failed to maintain its footing this year: soaring into 29th position last year, in the 2008/09 rankings it has not even placed within the top 500. It will be interesting to see if Facebook can keep its cool in 2009/10.

Equally it will be fascinating to see how iPhone performs next year. Occupying second place this year, it is a position held last year by a fellow Apple sub-brand, iPod – which dropped to 40th this year. Will Apple's 'next big thing' replace iPhone in the 2009/10 top 20? Or can two of Apple's sub-brands secure positions in the top 20? The parent brand itself glows in the limelight of its stylish and inventive products, rising another four places to rest in third position this year. However, does the fact that both iPod and iTunes dropped out of the top 20 hold any long term concerns for Apple?

Facebook and iPhone aside, the top 20 features many of the 'usual gang'. Perhaps the best illustration of the firm grip the brands have on their top 20 ranking can be seen in the fact that only seven of the current top 20 fell down the rankings at all; the biggest faller dropping a mere nine places, with that distinction going to PlayStation. Of last year's top 20, those that did not make the top group once again have also only slipped slightly, with just two (both internet-based brands) experiencing any notable fall: Amazon.co.uk, which has fallen to 80th place, and retail-come-auctioneer eBay, now 89th.

CATEGORY KILLERS

Despite the assumption that out of the three surveys The Centre for Brand Analysis (TCBA) conducts on behalf of Superbrands UK – namely CoolBrands, Superbrands (which looks at mass market consumer brands) and Business Superbrands (business to business brands) – the CoolBrands results would be likely to show the most volatility, it is actually the most static toward the top of the rankings. However, despite this consistency at the top, the overall survey continues to show immense variety and change.

As always, the brands in this survey cover a huge range of sectors with a total of 35 categories represented in the 2008/09 top 500. In this publication alone, we see a brand like wagamama sitting next to Williams F1, while Reggae Reggae Sauce rubs shoulders with the Roundhouse and Cambridge Audio features alongside Cirque du Soleil. You don't get much more diverse than that.

The best performing category, in terms of the volume of its brands featuring in the top 500, is Home Products & Furnishings. It contributes 31 brands, led by cooking equipment brand Le Creuset, which began trading back in 1925. The Fashion – Designer category follows with 28 brands, headed up by Italian giant Prada. Technology – General takes joint silver by virtue of also having 28 brands featured in the top 500, and is led, of course, by Apple. Other categories flourishing include both the Retail

TOP 10 CATEGORIES BY VOLUME

1	Home Products & Furnishings
2=	Fashion – Designer
2=	Technology – General
4	Retail
5	Fashion – Accessories, Jewellery & Watches
6	Toiletries – Skincare
7	Drinks – Spirits
8	Food
9	Leisure & Entertainment – Restaurants & Coffee Shops
10	Automotive – Cars

TOP 10 CATEGORIES BY AVERAGE POSITION

1	Technology – Telecommunications
2	Drinks – Champagne
3	Automotive – Cars
4	Leisure & Entertainment – UK Attractions & The Arts
5	Mobile Telecommunications
6	Media – Newspapers & Magazines
7	Online
8	Automotive – Motorbikes
9	Leisure & Entertainment – Games & Toys
10	Fashion – Designer

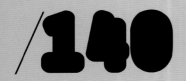

and the Fashion – Accessories, Jewellery & Watches segments. At the other end of the spectrum Financial Services adds just one brand to the official 500; a notable performance by first direct.

If we examine the categories represented in the top 500 another way, specifically by the average position attained by the brands from a given sector, a different set of categories comes to the fore. This measure, it can be argued, is a better gauge of exploring whether a sector achieves quality as opposed to quantity. Leading the way under this approach is the Technology – Telecommunications category. Its six brands average 104th place. The Drinks – Champagne category comes second, with brands averaging 116th place. The third best performing category (on this measure) is Automotive – Cars; its 18 entries (led by top CoolBrand Aston Martin) average 134th place. The three categories with the lowest average positions are Toiletries – Skincare, Fashion – Boutique Clothing, and Drinks – Spirits with average positions of 326th, 339th and 340th respectively.

In terms of how well categories have fared year-on-year in volume terms, Retail sees the strongest improvement, with 12 more brands making the top 500 this year. It is followed closely by the Drinks – Spirits category which has 11 more brands than in 2007/08. Some of the worst performing categories year-on-year in volume terms include Fashion – Designer (although despite this, it remains one of the largest sectors featured in the top 500), Media – Newspapers & Magazines, and Sportswear & Equipment.

INDIVIDUAL BRANDS

Casting aside the categories and looking more specifically at how individual brands have fared in terms of year-on-year performance, there are some very impressive improvements. Dorset Cereals is the biggest year-on-year riser within the 500, enhancing its position by 301 places. A resurgent Habitat has risen 284 places, while upmarket hotel Sanderson climbs by 252 places. Young brands, such as Beyond the Valley – which has continued its growth success with a rise of 235 positions – are joined by established brands such as British icon Rolls-Royce, which jumps up 180 places.

Just five brands perform consistently, maintaining the exact same position year-on-year: Agent Provocateur, Bang & Olufsen, Evian, Skype, and of course the number one brand Aston Martin. Three of these are in the overall top 10. Thirty-six brands maintain their position within five places, ranging from Seeds of Change and Louis Vitton to San Miguel and the Eden Project.

A range of brands have also experienced quite dramatic falls in the year-on-year rankings, topped by Rizla, which fell a substantial 278 places. Other notable fallers include the weekly women's magazine, Grazia, which has fallen 191 positions; mobile company Orange, which continues its downward trend by falling another 165 places; and, possibly suggesting the desire for an eco-friendly car has already waned, Smart Car tumbles 141 positions.

There are more than 180 new entries into the top 500, suggesting volatility is healthy in the list outside of the tight top 20. Some of the highest entries are Facebook in 19th position, Ray-Ban in 25th place, Sky+ in 58th and Tiffany in 50th position.

YEAR-ON-YEAR CLIMBERS

BRAND	RANK 2007/08	RANK 2008/09	IMPROVEMENT
Dorset Cereals	468	167	301
Habitat	390	106	284
Illy	434	182	252
Sanderson	431	179	252
Brabantia	437	196	241
Carluccio's	456	217	239
Beyond the Valley	465	230	235
Hotel du Vin	364	135	229
Bumble & Bumble	412	191	221
Shiseido	436	222	214
Storm	313	110	203
Land Rover	395	194	201
My by Myla	450	256	194
Issey Miyake	287	96	191
Malmaison	318	130	188
Bliss	496	309	187
L'Artisan Parfumeur	495	311	184
Wallpaper*	344	160	184
Patisserie Valerie	346	163	183
Rolls-Royce	280	100	180

WHO KNOWS?

As happened last year – and indeed the year before – there is a massive difference in the opinion of the Expert Council and the British consumers. This is perhaps to be expected but the size of the differing view is in some instances quite surprising.

In cases where a brand is extremely new, niche or exclusive, one might assume the council to be much more familiar with the brand, perhaps explaining the performance gap. For example the council places Soho House Group – the owners of the exclusive membership clubs and restaurants, as well as Cowshed – eighth in its rankings. This is a full 413 places above the consumer rank for the brand. You would, however, assume that not many of the consumers surveyed have necessarily visited or even heard of the brand. Another example might be the exclusive restaurant The Wolseley, which sits 535 places higher in the council ranking.

However, such gaps are not restricted to brands with which experts may be more familiar. Well-known brand Converse All Stars, for example, sits 155 places higher in the council vote than in that of consumers, while Topshop is rated 88 places higher by the council than by consumers. Even iPod is positioned a staggering 248 places higher by the council, showing that consumers have lost adoration for the MP3 far quicker than the experts.

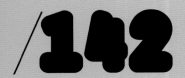

Conversely, the public love affair with the automotive sector is evident with five of its brands making the consumer top 10, led by Harley-Davidson. The iconic bike manufacturer comes out number one overall in the consumer vote, a full 559 places above its council ranking. Ferrari sits third in the consumer rankings, 133 places higher than in the council rankings, while Lamborghini in eighth and Porsche in ninth are both a full 207 places higher than their position in the council vote. Interestingly, Facebook isn't quite so in favour with the council – 16th in the consumer vote but 111 places lower in the council rankings.

Of course some brands that members of the public might not have directly owned or experienced, including Aston Martin, still perform strongly in the consumer vote and equally many populist brands still perform strongly with the council, so basic assumption cannot be made overall on the trends. Other factors need to be kept in mind, such as the emotional reaction these brands create. Aspiration, the excitement the brands incite, the sense of recognition and peer approval they instil, simple awareness levels and press coverage are just a few of the additional influences. Nevertheless, to illustrate the huge differences, only two brands make both the expert and consumer top 10.

	EXPERT TOP 20 2008/09	CONSUMER TOP 20 2008/09
1	Apple	Harley-Davidson
2	Aston Martin	Aston Martin
3	iPhone	Ferrari
4	iPod	iPhone
5	Christian Louboutin	Rolex
6	Marc Jacobs	Nintendo
7	Agent Provocateur	YouTube
8	Soho House Group	Lamborghini
9	Tate Modern	Porsche
10	Bang & Olufsen	Google
11	Leica	Dom Perignon
12	Manolo Blahnik	Bollinger
13	Converse All Stars	Diesel
14	The Wolseley	PlayStation
15	Balenciaga	Bang & Olufsen
16	Google	Facebook
17	Triumph	Jimmy Choo
18	Ducati	Apple
19	Topshop	Xbox
20	Frieze Art Fair	BlackBerry

THE SELECTION PROCESS

The selection process begins in earnest when researchers working for The Centre for Brand Analysis (TCBA) compile a list of brands operating in the UK. Unlike many other award schemes that exist, brands do not apply to be considered in the process. This initial list features thousands of brands. It is painstakingly created, drawing on sources ranging from consumer magazines, blogs and 'hot lists' to official market reports. Brands are also put forward by members of the public, through the CoolBrands website.

A range of sector specialists also help to feed into the initial list, to ensure it is as comprehensive as possible. This year journalists from magazines including Olive, Pure Beauty, The Grocer and Square Meal provided insight into their specific sectors, while experts from the likes of WGSN and marketing agencies such as Profero also contributed ideas.

Following this process, the list is narrowed down by TCBA to a more manageable version for consideration by the independent Expert Council. This year, the list considered by the council featured approximately 1,100 brands. As a final check any member of the council can add in brands that they think have been missed, which usually results in a few additions.

This year the size of the council was increased (as it had been in 2007/08 as well), principally adding opinion formers from different backgrounds. These ranged from Katrina Larkin, the co-founder of The Big Chill, to radio & TV broadcaster Lauren Laverne. Aside from opinion formers, a number of journalists were also added to the council for the first time. These included the editors of VOGUE.COM, Cosmopolitan.co.uk, fashion trade bible Drapers and the associate editor & director of health & beauty at Harper's Bazaar. In total, 19 of the 31 council members were new.

All the council members are voluntary and of course independent. Their role is to score the short list of brands based on their opinion of each entry's cool credentials. That is clearly a subjective process, although members have to bear in mind six core factors – style, innovation, originality, authenticity, desirability and uniqueness – when allocating their scores. They do not rate brands that they are unfamiliar with or any that they work with. These scores are collated and discussed in detail at a council meeting. Always generating a lively debate, a range of issues are addressed before the final scores and positions are agreed upon.

The lowest-scoring brands from this table (approximately 40 per cent) are eliminated from the process. A nationally representative group of more than 2,500 UK consumers, accessed via a YouGov panel, then vote on the surviving brands.

The council and consumer results are combined to create a final score – the expert opinion constitutes 70 per cent of the overall total and the consumer opinion 30 per cent. This weighting reflects the importance of opinion leaders in the cool space and their greater knowledge and awareness of these sometimes niche brands. The brands are then sorted by their score to create a ranking, with the top 500 deemed to be the CoolBrands.

THE TRUTH ABOUT COOL

NIKU BANAIE

**Vice President of
Strategy & Innovation
Isobar**

Isobar is the world's largest digital marketing network. Covering 38 markets and connecting some of the very best digital agencies, its services include strategy & consulting, web site build, online advertising & media, paid & organic search, social & viral marketing, CRM and mobile. A philosophy of 'Creativity, Collaborative Innovation and Agility' has earned it more creative awards in the last two years than any other digital network.

Remember Nathan Barley? Maybe you remember one of his more memorable quotes: 'Stupid people think it's cool, smart people think it's a joke – also cool.'

He was the main character in the self-titled 2005 Channel 4 sitcom, written by Charlie Brooker and Chris Morris. Wikipedia describes him as: 'A webmaster, guerrilla filmmaker, screenwriter, DJ and in his own words, a "self-facilitating media node". He is convinced he is the epitome of urban cool, and therefore secretly terrified he might not be, which is why he reads Sugar Ape magazine, his bible of cool.'

Nathan Barley satirized the lifestyles of many within the creative industries – marketing, design, fashion, film and especially those based in Shoreditch, east London. The show emerged during a time when large corporations would spend vast amounts of money in an effort to unearth 'the next big thing', hiring 'cool hunters' to go out and observe young people and report back their findings. Corporations believed that the quicker they could hit upon the essence of cool, the quicker they could package it up and sell it back to us – for profit.

There were several problems with this approach. Firstly, by the time the findings were distilled and reported back, things had often changed and moved on. Secondly, there was an assumption that cool was purely the reserve of young people within niche sub-cultures. Thirdly, and more fundamentally, many of the insights assumed 'cool equals style' and therefore created a time where companies were slaves to the fleeting whims of fashion and predications from the 'cool hunters'. The result? Products and services that made little impact on popular culture and had short-lived existences.

Outside of this world, however, were the companies and brands that did not even use the word 'cool' in their vocabulary; those which not only created their own path based on what they believed in, but which were brave enough to move forward without relying on research to tell them how to be cool. It is from this faction that the brands capable of making a real difference have emerged, a hotbed for the brands reaching the top of the CoolBrands list.

So, what can we learn from the top scoring brands like Apple, Tate Modern and Google? What truths exist to show us what makes them different?

To begin this investigation (an admittedly trivial one) we should start with the origins of the word. 'Cool' is an especially ubiquitous slang word that has become so generic and ambiguous that its meaning is hard to pin down. With the Oxford Dictionary definition leaving me un-satisfied, I discovered a whole range of cultural interpretations of cool.

Image courtesy of Aston Martin

The origin of the word can be traced back to Africa. Early West African tribes originally conceived the linguistic equivalent of cool as the most desirable state of being. In Robert Farris Thompson's 'An Aesthetic of the Cool', the Gola people of Liberia defined the term as "the ability to be nonchalant at the right moment ... to reveal no emotion ... it is particularly admirable to do difficult tasks with an air of ease and silent disdain".

The Italians have a term, 'sprezzatura', which is used to describe an effortless, artistic chic; most famously personified by Da Vinci's Mona Lisa and popular during the High Renaissance.

Then, after World War II came the concept of 'American Cool', born from the jazz and Beatnik countercultures; a time that saw the birth of

'the teenager' with a rebellious spirit, freedom after the war, and wealth. It was at this point that commerce began to commandeer cool, as the demographic of youth emerged as the marketing man's target of choice.

In 'Bohemia: Digging the Roots of Cool', author Herbert Gold writes: 'To be cool or hip meant hanging out pursuing sexual experiences, displaying the appropriate attitude of narcistic self-absorption, and expressing a desire to escape the mental straight jacket of all ideological causes. Back then cool was defined by an attitude of defiance and an expression of rebellion.'

What we learn by looking to the past is that the factors that make up cool will mutate from time to time, from place to place and from generation to generation.

Today, the brands that feature in the CoolBrands top 10 do not all follow one set of rules. On the contrary, it is the lack of cliché cool strategies that have got them to where they are today. We have success stories from the social media world (such as YouTube) which aren't designer, niche or aspirational. Instead they play to a generation's need to share, sometimes make interesting video content and maybe even become an internet star – this is 'cool as a democratic tool', delivering against the need for self-expression and connection in the online world.

Apple dominates the top 10 with a combination of its hardware and services (iPhone) alongside the experience of the Apple retail stores, itself more akin to an entertainment product than your average shop. This is 'cool as lifestyle utility',

allowing mainstream audiences to feel a sense of rebellion against the big bland machine that is Microsoft and part of one movement.

Then there is Aston Martin, which has remained in the top position for the last few years with its play on 'cool as elusive essence'. A truly aspirational product that, by design, has become more than a car and closer to a tool of sexual attraction for both men and women. One truth they all have in common is that none of them set out to be cool. By having a unique attitude and perspective, sense of momentum, and the ability to define the cultural zeitgeist, they have managed to become big cultural ideas in their own right.

The unique attitude and perspective is evident in Tate Modern, both though its approach to showing content and experiences but also in the way it communicates. It has remained true to itself and is constantly innovating in the way it brings art to the masses. Never simply sitting back, it continues to create new energy around contemporary art that subsequently defines a cultural moment in time and gets us all talking, whether it's Carsten Holler's slides or Doris Salcedo's magnificent subterranean chasm that stretched the length of the Turbine Hall.

It has its own style and has forged its own path like many of the brands in the list. People get behind ideas that

challenge the status quo, that are independent in spirit and that demonstrate real passion in what they do. What is great about these ideas is that they do not exclusively come from the edges of popular culture. Instead their power comes from being accepted universally by young people as well as older crowds; proving the point that cool is an attitude and not an exclusive youth phenomenon.

The belief that cool only happens with those at the bleeding edges of culture (usually the young) and then trickles down to the masses doesn't stand up in a connected 'Web 2.0' world. We are witnessing big ideas, like Google, that started from the centre (rather than the edge) now becoming all encompassing and not relying on the cliché that a recognised 'cool influencer' (from the edge) is required to initiate a positive ripple effect.

For those of you interested in theory you may want to Google the words 'Watts vs Gladwell'. Duncan Watts is a Professor of Sociology at Columbia University and a principle research scientist at Yahoo! while Malcolm Gladwell is an accomplished author ('The Tipping Point' and 'Blink') and staff writer for The New Yorker.

Gladwell believes that behind every trend lies a small group of tastemakers that act as a spark, which is subsequently picked up by less-cool people, and so on, until it goes mainstream. This is loosely referred to as the 'Influentials theory' and is the premise of viral and word-of-mouth campaigns in the advertising industry. Reach those rare super-influencers and you'll reach everyone else through them, for free.

Watts, on the other hand, has another idea. He has conducted a series of controversial experiments that challenge the Influentials model. By analysing email patterns, he found that highly connected people are not, in fact, crucial social hubs. He then wrote his own programs to track how rumours spread and discovered that the average Joe is just as likely to start a new trend as a well-connected individual. Finally, he demonstrated that the sudden success of a hot new band might actually be random. Any attempt to engineer success through Influentials, he argues, is almost certainly doomed to failure.

I'm afraid to conclude that the truth is, there is no perfect formula to create 'cool'. It can't simply be bought off the shelf (or from an agency, celebrity or cool hunter). My advice would be to ban the word from corporate boardrooms and instead to search deep inside the brand to uncover a unique point of view; only then will you even begin to stand apart from the pack.

MUSIC AND THE SCIENCE OF COOL

JACK HORNER

**Co-Founder & Creative Director
FRUKT**

FRUKT is the world's leading specialist music strategy and communications agency, facilitating a more creative and effective use of music by consumer brands. With a broad range of specialist marketing, communications and consumer insight expertise, the company works with both consumer brands and music companies to develop strategic partnerships and targeted campaigns.

THE BIG BANG

It's a new musical world out there. The catalyst of free online content has driven a stake through the heart of the old music world – cracking open those jewel cases and setting music free. Consumers are now demanding more from the music they love, especially as they realise that ownership is not the be all and end all of music consumption. This is 'Music 2.0': harder, better, stronger, faster. If you're still rocking 'Music 1.0', you might as well turn up to a gig wearing Bri-Nylon trousers, clutching your pipe and slippers. The old way of experiencing music simply just isn't cool anymore.

THE MUSICAL DAWN OF MAN

In the beginning was the word, and the word was… well, a bit dull on its own. So Adam and Eve made a drum from some nearby snakeskin and gave birth to music, and the rest, as they say, is history. OK, maybe I've embellished the facts slightly here, but the overriding message is simple – music has always been with us. Since that first caveman banged out a tribal beat, our obsession with music has been innate – there is an overwhelming, uncontrollable desire, which draws us to music and the things that surround it. Martin Lindstrom's

2005 book, 'Brand Sense', estimated that 83 per cent of all marketing communication is limited to sight alone. However, it also pointed to a 65 per cent chance of a mood change when exposed to a positive sound. Which begs the question: can your consumers hear you?

REWRITING THE HISTORY BOOKS

Casting a retrospective glance at the annals of music's rich history, we can trace four distinct processes in its evolution. First music was personal, a tune for the sake of a tune amongst friends – storytelling set to sound. Then, as music started the long road that would eventually lead to commercialisation, it became something to be enjoyed 'over there' – as live music (whether it was for the court of kings or street buskers amongst the great unwashed) became something of a spectator sport for the many. Then with the arrival of the 'musical printing press' that was wax cylinders, records and then CDs, music became something tangible for the first time – you could touch it, hold in your hand, own it, and play it at will. Now in the fourth regeneration of music, with all the technological advances, numerous musical genres, and the creation of recording empires built on sound, music has done a very strange thing: it's returned to the start of the game. It's become personal again. The traditional recording industry suggests a piracy snake is at fault here, which has taken us back to square one, but in reality to quote The Lion King, it's all part of the musical "circle of life".

MUSIC IS BIGGER ON THE INSIDE

Music is big. Really big. To see it properly, it's best viewed on three levels:

1. Scale: Music is vast in its depth and breadth of content, genres and styles; and it is, much like the universe itself, constantly expanding. However, despite its seemingly infinite permeations, music is inclusive – there is something there for everyone.

2. Experience: Music is scalable across a broad myriad of platforms. It's not a cappella – it's an orchestra of multi-faceted opportunity. Just as there are many genres, there are also numerous ways of connecting to consumers via music, whether it's an integrated sponsorship opportunity, supporting artist discovery, or creating original interactive experiences.

3. Emotion: It's also big because of the amount of emotional value it carries. Music is all things to all people: the jogging soundtrack that makes a weary businessman briefly feel 15 again, the tear on a pillow of a teenage girl, the

Image © Dan Wilton

roar of a crowd, a trigger for a distant memory, the shared experience of 'being there' at a live gig.

The word 'cool' is a fairly abstract term, but at the heart of it is a strong element. Signs of the Time, a research institute studying 'cool' a few years ago, found one common denominator – cool is about empowerment. Ultimately, no matter what type of value we assign to our clothes and the objects we surround ourselves with, it's all about not feeling weak, ordinary, and alone. Cool is representational; it's how we want to be perceived by others. And music has the ability to help us be heard, to stand out in a crowd, to find our place, to sign up to what we believe in and what we want to be seen to be believing in. The term 'cool by association' has been bandied around as a fairly

negative term; in reality, brands have the option to be 'cool by integration' by putting music at the heart of their campaigns.

Studying the top 500 CoolBrands in detail reveals that more than 40 per cent of them have utilised the cool cache that music brings to their advantage, with at least 50 per cent of that figure putting music at the core of their brand's focus.

1/TECHNOLOGY

Apple, despite constructing solid products, spent a long time as the understudy to Microsoft. That was until it put music centre-stage. The iPod, now so ubiquitous, was the turning point for Apple. However, the brand was lifted

head and shoulders above Microsoft not just on the basis of its era-defining device, but also on the music that surrounded it. Apple has championed both megastars and launched the careers of small independent acts since 2001, to the point where the music from a new Apple advert is as anticipated and chart-affecting as the Levi's commercials of the 1980s and 1990s. From The Ting Tings, Feist, and CSS, Apple has made music the focal point of both its business and its core image. Microsoft doesn't make the CoolBrands list. However, the UK is still awaiting the launch of its Zune music player, while its Xbox line, which does feature in the list, is enjoying continuing success thanks, in part, to music via the ever-popular Guitar Hero franchise.

2/MOBILE

The big guns in the mobile industry have also been quick to sign up to the new music manifesto. Nokia, the largest handset manufacturer in the world, has recognised the value music can bring across a myriad of different platforms. Whether it's the creation of a direct iTunes competitor (Nokia Music Store), large-scale concert venues (Nokia LA Live), or online platforms promoting developing acts across Asia (Independent Artists Club), music has a vital role to play. Sony Ericsson, Samsung and LG are all also brands in the top 500 who are constantly seeking reinvention via music. The operators, too, know just how key music is to bridge the gap and make a somewhat ethereal and impersonal service tangible. O2 has leveraged its cool factor by building key properties around music, from the Wireless Festival right through to its groundbreaking venue, The O2 (which transformed the Millennium Dome into London's, and arguably one of the world's, most successful music venues). O2's brand name is now synonymous with the heart of London's music scene; cool doesn't come much more tangible than that.

3/FASHION

Levi's wouldn't be the brand it is today without 'I Heard It Through The Grapevine' (and Nick Kamen in his undies), and the brand still recognises the power of music today, to the point of setting up the Levity record label in Australia. Fashion, by its very nature, has always thrived off the back of its music associations and brands such as Topman, H&M, Gap and Diesel know that its audience is dressing to fit a lifestyle driven by their favourite sounds. The major names in footwear – Nike, adidas, Converse, and PUMA – may all have their heritage on the sports bench, but the lifestyle associations are now firmly rooted in music. Converse's 'Connectivity' campaign transcended various genres by combining Santogold, Pharrell Williams and Julian Casablancas to create a bespoke track, and it did so by giving the artists free reign. Converse is currently the shoe of choice

Image courtesy of Beck's, 2007

among indie musicians, and Dr Martens is also taping into its musical heritage; their days as a baseball sneaker or solid work shoe long gone as they reposition as essential music lifestyle accessories.

4/DRINKS

From pop to alcohol, music is at the forefront of the drinks brands' agenda. Jack Daniel's, one of the CoolBrands, is virtually a rock institution in its own right. Being on 'The Coke Side of Life' or in an 'Absolut World' means making the most out of

musical alignments and artist collaborations. Alcohol brands which have existed primarily on the basis of pouring rights at music festivals are realising that true integration with their consumers' passion points means taking a big leap for brand kind. Beck's, in the CoolBrands top 500, is a case in point. The brand has embarked on Beck's Fusions, creating bespoke events, which merge music (from the likes of Massive Attack and The Chemical Brothers) and art together. Coca-Cola, too, is actively promoting collaborative work between designers and musicians from

a global remit in its current 'WE08' Olympics campaign – where songs are created around tailor-made bottles. The emphasis here is on 'unique' experiences, bringing a 'cool' refreshing taste before a drop of liquid even passes a consumer's lips.

A SOLID GROUNDING IN MUSIC

As Isaac Newton discovered, in order to make that concerted gravitational hit with consumers, you need to be the apple – not the owner of the tree. Standing next to someone cool doesn't make you cool yourself by default. In order for brands to stand shoulder-to-shoulder with consumers, they need to integrate themselves with music, not just be the pores through which music is absorbed. Get stuck in, in the mosh pit, in the teenager's garage practicing a riff, on the businesswoman's morning commute, sharing, learning, and singing along. Music is a constant, capturing the zeitgeist of every passing generation. It's time to utilise the full capability of music's rich heritage and its ability to cerate touch points with target audiences of all ages.

In short, 'cool' isn't easily defined by words or actions. It's not an exact science, and there is no straightforward equation to follow.

However, I can tell you this – it has a cracking soundtrack.

CLUSTA

We are a design agency who have been producing award-winning, graphic and digital communications for more than 10 years.

Our experience combined with our knowledge allows us to produce world class design using cutting-edge techniques across multiple formats.

Our passion for design transcends expectations and creative dialogue is key to our process.

Client List
Publicis & Hal Riney
Discovery Channel
R/GA
Polydor
Ogilvy
Ordnance Survey
Umbro International
Pioneer
Carphone Warehouse
Birmingham City University
Sony BMG / Columbia
Pacha London
Steve Lawler
Cuban Brothers
Danny Howells
Agency.com
RPM

Telephone
+44 (0) 121 604 00041

Email
hello@clusta.com

Web
www.clusta.com

Clusta

QUALIFYING COOLBRANDS

123

42Below

A
A Bathing Ape
A Butcher of Distinction
Abel & Cole
Abercrombie & Fitch
Absolut
Acne Jeans
Acqua di Parma
Adidas
Aga
Agent Provocateur
Alessi
Alexander McQueen
Alfa Romeo
All Saints
Amazon.co.uk
American Apparel
Anna Sui
Anya Hindmarch
Apple
Aprilia
Asahi
Asia de Cuba
Asos.com
Aston Martin
Atari
Audi
Aveda

B
B&B Italia
Balenciaga
Bang & Olufsen
Bar Italia
Barbican Centre
Barbour
Bebo
Beck's
Belu
Ben & Jerry's
Benefit
Bentley
Berghaus
Beyond Retro
Beyond the Valley
BFI Southbank
Billionaire Boys Club
Biotherm
Birkenstock
BlackBerry
Blaupunkt
Bliss

BMW
Bobbi Brown
Bodum
Boffi
Bollinger
Bombay Sapphire
Bose
Botanics
Brabantia
Breil
British Airways
Browns
BSA
Buddhistpunk
Budweiser Budvar
Bulthaup
Bumble & Bumble
Burberry
Burton Snowboards
Burt's Bees
Busaba Eathai

C

Cambridge Audio
Campari
Camper
Canon
Carhartt
Carluccio's
Chanel
Chantecaille
Chivas Regal
Chloé
Christian Louboutin
Church's
Cirque du Soleil
Clarins
Clinique
Cobra Beer
Coca-Cola
Coco Ribbon
Comme des Garçons
Connect 4
Converse All Stars
Copella
Corona
COS
Courvoisier
Creative Review
Crème de la Mer
Cutler and Gross

D

Damaris
Daylesford Organic
Dazed & Confused

DC Comics
Decléor
De'Longhi
Denon
Dermalogica
Design Hotels
Design Museum
Diesel
Diptyque
Disaronno
Dolby
Dom Perignon
Dorset Cereals
Dr Hauschka
Dr Martens
Dr Sebagh
Dries Van Noten
Ducati

E

EA
EBay
Eden Project
Elemis
Elle Macpherson Intimates
Eurostar
Eve Lom
Evian
Evisu
Expedia.co.uk

F

Facebook
Falke
Farmacia Urban Healing
Farrow & Ball
Feather & Black
Fender
Ferrari
Fever-Tree
Figleaves.com
Fiji Natural Artesian Water
Finlandia
Firebox.com
First Direct
Fish
Flickr
Fortnum & Mason
Four Seasons Hotels
   and Resorts
Fred Perry
Frieze Art Fair
Fudge

G

G-Star Raw
Gaggenau
Gaggia
Gap
Gaydar.co.uk
Ghd
Gibson
Gio-Goi
Givenchy
Global Knives
Google
Gordon Ramsay
Gourmet Burger Kitchen
GQ
Graham & Green
Grazia
Green & Black's
Greenwich Village
Grey Goose
Grolsch
Gü
Gucci
Guerlian
Guinness

H

H&M
Häagen Dazs
Habitat
Hakkasan
Hamleys
Harley-Davidson
Harman Kardon
Harriet's Muse
Harrods
Harvey Nichols
Havaianas
Havana Club
Heal's
Hendricks
Hennessy
Hermès
Hip Hotels
Hoegaarden
Holy Moly
Hotel Chocolat
Hotel du Vin
Howies

I

ICA
Illy
Imax
Innocent

IPhone
IPod
Issey Miyake
Itsu

J

Jack Daniel's
Jaguar
Jean Paul Gaultier
Jelly Belly
Jimmy Choo
Jo Malone
John Frieda
John Smedley
Johnnie Walker
Jonathan Saunders
Joseph

K

Kawasaki
Kef
Kenzo
Kérastase
Kettle Chips
Kiehl's
King of Shaves
KitchenAid
Konami
Korres
Krug
Krups
Kurt Geiger

L

La Perla
La Prairie
Lab Series
Lacoste
Lamborghini
Lancôme
Land Rover
Lara Bohinc
L'Artisan Parfumeur
Last.fm
Laura Mercier
Lavazza
Le Creuset
Leatherman
Leffe
Leica
Levi's
LG
Liberty
Ligne Roset
Linda Farrow Vintage
Linn

/155

Locanda Locatelli
Loewe
London Eye
Lonely Planet
Lotus
Louis Vuitton
Lovefilm.com
LSA
Lulu Guinness
Lyle & Scott

MAC
McLaren
Madame V
Maglite
Magners
Malmaison
Mandarina Duck
Manolo Blahnik
Mappin & Webb
Marc Jacobs
Marharishi
Marks & Spencer
Marmite
Marni
Marshall
Marvel Comics
Mercedes-Benz
Miele
Mini
Modern Toss
Moët & Chandon
MOP
Mr & Mrs Smith
Muji
My by Myla
MyHotels

Narciso Rodriguez
Nars
Neal's Yard Dairy
Neal's Yard Remedies
Neff
Net-A-Porter
New Balance
New Covent Garden
 Food Co.
Nike
Nikon
Nintendo
Nobu
Nokia
Nude Skincare
Nudie Jeans Co.

O2
O'Neill
Oakley
Ocado
Oki-Ni
Oliver Goldsmith
Oliver Peoples
Olympus
Omega
One Aldwych
Onitsuka Tiger
Orange
Origins
Osborne & Little

Panasonic
Patek Philippe
Patisserie Valerie
Patron Tequila
Paul Smith
Peekaboo Vintage
Peroni Nastro Azzurro
Perrier
Piaggio
Pimm's
Pink
Pioneer
PJ Smoothies
Planet Organic
Play.com
PlayStation
Poggenpohl
Pol Roger
Pomegreat
Pop
Porsche
PPQ
Prada
Premier Model Management
Prescriptives
Primark
Princesse Tam Tam
Prius
Puma
Purves & Purves

Rachel's Organic
Ralph Lauren
Range Rover
Ray-Ban
Raymond Weil
Reggae Reggae Sauce

Reiss
Remy Martin
REN
Rigby & Peller
Rizla
Roberto Cavalli
Roberts Radio
Roc
Rococo Chocolates
Roka
Roland
Rolex
Rolls-Royce
Rough Guides
Rough Trade
Roundhouse
Rubik's Cube
Ruby & Millie
Rude Health

S. Pellegrino
Saab
Saatchi Gallery
Samsonite
Samsung
San Miguel
Sanderson
Scalextric
ScooterMan
Scott's
Scrabble
Seeds of Change
Select Model Management
Selfridges
Sennheiser
Shiseido
Singapore Airlines
Size?
SK-II
Skinny Cow
Sky+
Skylon
Skype
Smart Car
Smeg
Smirnoff
Smythson of Bond Street
Soho House Group
Sony
Sony Ericsson
Space NK
Specialized
St Martins Lane
STA Travel
Staropramen
Stella McCartney

Stephen Webster
Stila
Stolichnaya
Storm
Streetcar
Stussy
Suzuki
Swarovski

Tablet Hotels
Tag Heuer
Tanqueray
Tate Modern
Tatty Devine
Taylor Taylor
The Cinnamon Club
The Conran Shop
The Designers Republic
The Dispensary
The Fat Duck
The Glenlivet
The Guardian/The Observer
The Halkin
The Hoxton Hotel
The Independent/The
 Independent on Sunday
The Ivy
The Laden Showroom
The Lowry
The Lowry Hotel
The Metropolitan
The North Face
The O2
The Old Vic
The Organic Pharmacy
The Times/The Sunday Times
The Wapping Project
The White Company
The Wolseley
The Zetter
Thierry Mugler
Thom Browne
Tiffany
Tiger Beer
Time Out City Guides
Tod's
Tom Ford
TomTom
Top Trumps
Topman
Topshop
Trailfinders
Trip Advisor
Triumph
Twinings
Tyrrells

Ugg
Uniqlo
Urban Junkies
Urban Outfitters
Urban Splash

Vaio
Vanity Fair
Vans
Vespa
Veuve Clicquot
Villeroy & Boch
Virgin Atlantic
Vitra
Vivienne Westwood
Vogue
Vox
VV Rouleaux

W Hotels
Wagamama
Wahl
Waitrose
Wallpaper* City Guides
Wembley Stadium
Wharfedale
Whole Foods Market
Wikipedia
Williams F1
Wolford
Wrangler
Wyborowa

Xbox

Yamaha
Yauatcha
YMC
Yo Sushi!
Yotel
YouTube
YSL

Zara
Zippo